The Student and the Learning Environment

Susan S. Meihofer,
Editor

National Education Association
Washington, D.C.

CONTENTS

Introduction 5

THE INDIVIDUAL STUDENT

Physical Fitness: A Cornerstone of Learning 7
Paul Hunsicher

Mental Fitness: A Prime Factor in Learning 13
Robert F. Peck and James V. Mitchell, Jr.

Anxiety: A Deterrent to Effective Learning 23
Frederick F. Lighthall

Motivation: An Initiation to the Learning Process 34
Don E. Hamachek

Creativity: An Extension of the Learning Parameters .. 46
E. Paul Torrance

THE CLASSROOM GROUP

The Group: An Asset or a Liability to Learning? 58
Louis M. Smith

Group Interaction: A Significant Force in Learning .. 68
Jean D. Grambs

Disadvantaged Groups: A Special Challenge 81
Gertrude Noar

THE LEARNING ENVIRONMENT

The Sensory Environment: A Building Block to Learning 94
G. F. McVey

Listening: A Particular Sensory Concern............ 104
Stanford E. Taylor

Media: A Current and Future Environment 114
Gerald M. Torkelson

Directed Study: A Commitment of Home and School
    to Learning 126
Ruth Strang

Discipline: A Maintenance of a Learning Environment . 133
William J. Gnagey

Susan S. Meihofer, the editor of this book, is a writer and editor of text materials. She holds an ETM from Harvard University Graduate School of Education.

INTRODUCTION

The selections in this book discuss a wide variety of elements that enhance or inhibit the learning process, from areas of individual physical and mental health to the teaching media available in the classroom. Throughout the book the individual student is viewed in relation to the classroom or sociological group, the teacher, and/or the conditions of the classroom environment. Many of the authors offer the teacher suggestions for altering the classroom environment to improve the possibilities for learning, as well as for understanding the interactions of the student with student and student with group.

The articles have been organized around three major themes: The Individual Student; the Classroom Group; and The Learning Environment, in order that their content might be as accessible as possible to educator and general reader alike. Read in any order, however, the individual selections should prove helpful to any teacher who wishes to establish optimum conditions for learning, both in the classroom and in the wider environment of each student.

Physical Fitness: A Cornerstone of Learning

by Paul Hunsicher

DEFINITIONS OF FITNESS

The term "physical fitness" has been used to denote many things and, as a result, has created confusion in the public mind as well as in professional ranks. The lack of a clear-cut, precise definition serves as a stumbling block when actually it need not be one. Engineers did marvelous things with electricity without knowing precisely what it was. But perhaps it will help to look at some of the interpretations of physical fitness currently in use.

Fitness as Freedom from Disability and Disease

The armed forces generally consider a person physically fit for service if she/he is free from any pathological condition and devoid of any physical disability. This definition is quite different from the one held by professional physical educators. While the former takes no cognizance of the state of *training* of the individual, the physical educator has taken a keen interest in this aspect of the subject. In physical education, "freedom from disease" is a point of departure for building up physical fitness through a training program.

Fitness as Available Energy

Physical fitness in terms of available energy sometimes is called "biodynamic potential." The fit person is capable of performing prolonged work. She/he can meet the physical demands of a daily routine and possesses sufficient reserve for additional activities.

The thought that through *energy expenditure* the individual builds up more potential energy should interest every adult. The acquisition and maintenance of energy reserves is one of the key factors in the whole physical fitness problem. Living a full life demands more than just staying alive, and nothing is quite as pathetic as the old person with insufficient energy reserve to enjoy life. Physical effort and health are means whereby we acquire the extra energy associated with a high state of fitness.

MANY FACTORS IN PHYSICAL FITNESS

The subject of physical fitness has many ramifications, and the classroom teacher interested in this subject needs to become aware of many aspects. The following paragraphs, particularly germane and pertinent to the topic, should be helpful. Physical fitness is composed of many components and attributes. A partial list would include body strength, muscular endurance, agility, cardiorespiratory efficiency, speed, balance, and flexibility.

While everyone possesses agility, strength, and other characteristics to some extent, individuals may have a high degree of one component and a relatively low degree of another. In other words, the interrelationships between components of physical fitness may not be particularly high. This is analogous to saying that a person may have a defective digestive system and still possess an efficient brain. Obviously, the most fit person is the one who has the greatest number of desirable qualities in the largest quantity.

A second important concept is that physical fitness exists in varying degrees, and practically any person can improve on her/his present state. You may think of one person who is just above the "freedom from disease" level at one end of a scale and, at the other extreme, the Olympic distance runner. An individual can be placed on this scale largely as a reflection of the amount of training she/he has been exposed to. The important point for the teacher is that practically all students can improve their status if they are willing to exert the energy.

Fitness Requires Physical Activity

While food provides the chief basis of energy, to raise the energy potential of an individual, the person must *expend* energy. One does not train an individual for a marathon race by making more food available. Rather *You run her/him.* There is no "royal road" to top-flight physical condition, and everyone who aspires to a higher level of fitness must be prepared to pay the price of expending additional energy. The key to greater energy reserve is through energy expenditure. The training regimes of distance runners, paratroopers, and infantry rangers are strenuous so as to condition them for the tasks ahead. Every single program has one common factor, namely, a high expenditure of human energy.

Fitness a Lifelong Possibility

While physical fitness may be highest during a relatively few years of a person's life, it should be emphasized that age alone is not the determining factor. Training is of far greater importance, and it is a matter of record that some athletes have remained active well beyond middle age. One authority succinctly summarized this concept in his remark, "At least one aspect of aging, the decline of efficiency, can be inhibited by 25 years and more provided there is systematic and lasting application of suitable physical training."

Even the individual not interested in sports as a career can benefit from a regular exercise program. Research workers have concluded that exercise can aid in preserving youthful body contours and maintaining organic vigor and the general resiliency of the body. At the other end of the scale, research workers have demonstrated that there is a rapid rate of muscular atrophy resulting from prolonged bed rest and disuse of muscles. Although hereditary factors play their part, there is little doubt that regular physical activity throughout life will delay the onset of degenerative conditions associatied with aging. When one realizes that ever-larger proportions of school children will attain the age of 70 in the future than in the past, it becomes increasingly important that all of them be made aware of the need for continuing an exercise program throughout life.

THE MEASUREMENT OF PHYSICAL FITNESS

Although a single definition for physical fitness is not available, many tests have been developed which measure some components of fitness. One could subdivide these into two categories—those tests taken in the resting or quiet state and those taken with the subject going through physical performances. Both have value.

Measuring Physical Status

Under the first category, such factors as the presence of pathology, the subject's weight, body build, vision, hearing, and posture would be tested. Ideally, the point of departure for any fitness program is the medical examination. Since all physical fitness programs involve physiological stress, it is imperative that the absence of pathology be confirmed prior to strenous physical activity.

Almost all agree that the classroom teacher and the school nurse are in a strategic position to note conditions which should be referred to a physician. Whether the examination is by the school physician or the family physician, the necessary facts on an unusual condition should be made known to the teacher. The classroom teacher is not responsible for diagnosis of and decisions on a student's health status, but the teacher must be advised how the child's health status is to be related to the physical fitness program.

Measuring Physical Activity

While the previously mentioned tests of physical fitness are necessary, teachers are also concerned with "people in action." Body movement is the *essential element* in physical education. Tests which indicate how well the girl or boy is able to function are indispensable when evaluating physical fitness. The teacher of physical education, in particular, is interested in knowing how well the student can run, jump, throw, and climb. These activities are expressions of strength, endurance, speed, agility, and neuromuscular coordination of the student. They represent the vehicles for achieving the various objectives of physical education.

In the development of physical fitness tests over the years, common practice has been to fractionate the components of fitness or parts of the body and design tests for each part. The teacher seeking a test of physical fitness should have little difficulty, since a number of agencies, both government and private, as well as individual research workers have developed test batteries.

A Few Cautions on Measurement

Virtually none of the short test batteries (three or four test items) will adequately measure all the components of fitness. However, this does not mean the tests are useless. A similar situation exists in the field of medical examinations. The average medical examination for insurance purposes may be less searching than the type of probing and clinical analyses characterizing the complete examination given at a hospital. Both examinations have value, but in the first instance the doctor would have to preface her/his remarks regarding the patient's state of health with caution because of limited information available. Time, money, and need may limit the type of medical examination given. Administrative considerations of this kind also have to be considered in the development of a physical fitness test. The important lesson for teachers is *to know what a given test measures and to limit their conclusions to the information obtained.*

The teacher should have some orientation ragarding the use of test norms. Despite what a few teachers think, pupils as well as parents are interested in knowing how their performance compares with a peer group. In fact, when students finish a test they frequently ask, "How good is that?" What they really want to know is how do their performances compare with those of other students.

While the typical student is interested in comparing test scores with those of others, she/he should be encouraged to compare her/his score with her/his own previous performance. The lure of competing against oneself is obvious from the number of golfers or bowlers who strive continually to break the previous scores they have made. An encouraging aspect of physical fitness stems from the fact that the vast majority of people can improve if they are willing to apply themselves.

Even though norms and standards serve a real function and are useful in teaching individuals, a word of caution regarding their use is appropriate. Do not set standards for a young person that are virtually impossible for the individual to meet. The result may be frustrating and could be mentally or physically harmful. Students should be stretched but not snapped.

The measurement of physical fitness is an obligation of the teacher of physical education. It is equally important that systematic records be kept, even if the students themselves maintain the records. The record forms should provide space for entering periodic test results so that the students have a longitudinal record of their changes in fitness. In addition to keeping students posted, the parents also should know how their children are progressing. The composite record of all students should be compiled annually for the principal, the superintendent, health experts, and others concerned with development of the curriculum. If this systematic study of procedures and results is made over a period of years, physical education will take its rightful place in the total educational plan.

SUMMARY

In recapitulation, it can be stated that the potential for a high level of physical fitness in our youth is present, but comparative studies indicate a need for further development. Physical fitness is more than freedom from disease. The added energy reserve of the fit person is important because it enables her/him to participate in many enjoyable pursuits.

A person is more attractive when fit than when unfit. Physical fitness is a lifetime proposition, and a fitness program can be started at any age level. Physical fitness can and should be measured, and the pupil should be apprised of her/his level of fitness.

Programs for developing physical fitness must take cognizance of three factors: rest, diet, and exercise. Many activities contribute to the development of physical fitness, and all that make a significant contribution involve a high energy expenditure.

Programs for developing physical fitness should be planned and should be both challenging and geared to the needs and capacities of the students.

Mental Fitness: A Prime Factor in Learning

by Robert F. Peck and James V. Mitchell, Jr.

Until quite recently, the term *mental health* brought to almost everyone's mind the vision of mental illness or of personality disturbance so serious as to cripple the individual's effectiveness. The notion that mental health concerns "crazy people," or that only peculiar people would seek education or self-development in the art of living, makes it difficult to win full acceptance and support for needed mental health services in our schools.

WHAT IS MENTAL HEALTH?

Recently a growing effort has been made to redefine mental health in positive terms. Among the positive characteristics that have been identified by numerous experts in the field are the following:

1. *Objective judgment:* the ability to look at all kinds of facts squarely and accurately, neither overlooking some nor exaggerating others. This ability is also called rationality, good sense, and even common sense.

2. *Autonomy:* the ability to deal with daily events in a self-starting, self-directing manner. Such terms as initiative, self-direction, and emotional independence are often used to convey this idea.

3. *Emotional maturity:* the ability to react to events with emotions which are appropriate in kind and in degree to the objective nature of the situation.

4. *Self-realizing drive:* the habit of working hard and purposefully to one's full capacity. People vary greatly in their physical, intellectual, and social potentialities, but it is possible to see in each case how far the given individual is putting his own particular potentialities to work to achieve personally worthwhile results. A person's powers, of course, are delimited by the state of her/his development. They are shaped by the opportunities she/he has had as well as by her/his innate potentialities.

5. *Self-acceptance:* a positive, self-respecting attitude toward one's self. Conscious self-insight or self-understanding may not be absolutely essential to an attitude of self-acceptance, but either seems to enhance considerably the objectivity and the wisdom of a person's self-regard.

6. *Respect for others:* a positive, acceptant attitude toward other people.

THE PSYCHOSOCIAL WORLD OF THE SCHOOL

There is some research on the influence of the total world of the school on the mental health and morale of its various members. From this, and from analogous studies of business organizations, it is possible to discern a few relationships between the human environment of a school and the development of its pupils.

Varied Human Relationships

The mental health of a child is affected by several sets of people in the school system. The influence of a student's immediate experience with the classroom teacher is obvious. What children know, but adults often forget, is that the school principal and the school janitor weigh potently in the minds of children, too. The principal may not even be present, or may be known only by very occasional contacts, but the attitudes and behavior she/he shows, or is reputed to show, color the school atmosphere for the children. Another set of people who have a profound impact on the child are his agemates. Perhaps the attitudes and values of agemates are second to the teacher's in influence in the primary grades, but by high school they outweigh the teacher's influence.

As many classroom teachers can testify, a second powerful influence for good or ill is the nature of the relationship the teacher has with a class or classes. Groups vary tremendously in their attitudes toward schoolwork and in their agreeableness or disagreeableness as a group. Their cohesiveness, or lack of it, can strongly affect the satisfaction and self-respect of the teacher.

A third factor is the kind of relationships among the teachers in a school. In many instances, these are casual enough so that they do not impinge sharply on the feelings or emotional stability of an individual teacher. However, there are schools in which warring factions create chronic tension and unpleasant dissension that adversely affect many of the faculty. There are other schools where it is a positive joy to work because of a friendly, stimulating, and agreeable atmosphere.

A fourth set of relationships are those which exist between the school staff and the board of education, and between the staff and the less formalized, but often strongly influential, power groups in the community. The relatively few studies which have tried to get objective measures of teacher morale, teacher turnover, community power structure, and the other strands of the web that makes up the psychosocial world of the school all demonstrate the powerful impact of community opinion on the morale and efficiency of teachers.

THE MENTAL HEALTH OF THE PUPIL

The dimensions of positive mental health that have been stated are, in a sense, the outcomes of healthy experiences. Moreover, these dimensions can be identified with some assurance because they appear to stem from the inherent needs of human beings. A. H. Maslow has suggested that the basic needs of the individual can be divided into five categories: (a) physiological needs, (b) safety needs, (c) love needs, (d) esteem needs, and (e) the need for self-actualization. These needs, as listed above, are conceived as hierarchial in organization, with the satisfaction of all prior needs a necessary prerequisite to the fulfillment of any one of them. Thus, self-actualization is very difficult to achieve unless the physiological, safety, love, and esteem needs have all been satisified within the context of everyday living. Such needs are not only applicable to adults; they are equally, if not more, demanding for children, who must learn socially acceptable ways of fulfilling them while coping with all the insecurities of growing up.

The Home as a Source of Need-Fulfillment

For each of the five needs listed above, the home has a crucial contribution to make to mental health. The fulfillment of the "safety" needs is a case in point. The safety needs are those whose fulfillment results in physical and emotional security for the child. One of the most important tasks of early infancy is the child's development of a basic and pervasive trust in parents that will permit some certainty and predictibility in part of life even though much of the individual's learning and growth will be fraught with uncertainties. This early need is extended into childhood and even into adolescence, when home is often seen as the one sure refuge against the complexities and challenges of a difficult period of growing up.

The typical child needs to have limits set on behavior, for without such limits the child becomes anxious and confused about the kind of behavior that is expected and approved. It is not only important that the limits be set, however, but that they be set *consistently,* for consistency of discipline contributes significantly to the child's sense of order about the world. All these are important contributions to the fulfillment of the safety needs.

The home is also of central importance in helping the child fulfill the needs for love and affection. Studies of children who are deprived of this all-important kind of need-fulfillment indicate that this handicap has severe negative repercussions for all aspects of development, including the physical, mental, and emotional. Apathy and emotional unresponsiveness are the symptoms of severe deprivation. Lesser degrees of deprivation can produce children who are fearful of close human relationships, who have lost the desire to please and to fulfill cultural expectations, who are resentful or even hostile toward authority figures, or who withdraw into a fantasy world as a reaction to their rejection.

A secure affectional relationship is a blessed gift to any child not only because it facilitates and enhances the living, loving, and growing processes of the child and makes them all seem more worthwhile but also because it leads ultimately to a close identification with one or both parents. This identification is most important for the child's development. From it, the child obtains a concrete guide to expected behavior; she/he gradually learns an appropriate sex role; and she/he achieves a sense of belonging and importance that develops self-confidence and eagerness to accept the new experiences and challenges of growing up.

It is unlikely that good mental health can be achieved without the fulfillment, also, of the need for self-esteem, the fourth need in Maslow's hierachy. Just as the love needs are closely related to the safety needs, and in fact need them as a foundation, so are the esteem needs closely related to and dependent on the fulfillment of the affectional needs. In the course of growing up, each child develops a "self-concept," which is simply an over-all perception of individual capabilities, strengths and weaknesses, future promise—a perception of the kind of person she/he really is. This self-concept develops from an interpretation of the reactions of others to oneself as a person. The reactions of those closest to the child naturally have the greatest influence. Thus, parents exercise preeminent influence on the developing self-concept of the child. If they show confidence, treat her/him as a worthy person, and demonstrate a generally approving attitude, the child's self-concept will soon incorporate self-confidence, a sense of personal worth, and a generally positive attitude toward herself/himself. This self-concept becomes increasingly firm, or less flexible, with age.

The School's Unique Role in Self-Fulfillment

At the pinnacle of the Maslow hierachy of needs is the need for self-actualization, which can be defined as the desire for self-fulfillment, or the tendency of the individual to want to bring her/his potential to fruition. Assisting the child along the rocky road to self-actualization is probably the most important single function of parenthood and of teaching. It calls for correspondingly great skills. Creative teaching, like creative parenthood, acknowledges the supreme importance of need-fulfillment in this area. Its practitioners make careful observations of a child's developing abilities and skills and provide appropriate experiences at just the right times. These are not the ones who force-feed experiences before the child is ready. They are the teachers who are on hand with exciting and worthwhile experiences when the time is ripe. Such teachers recognize the importance of encouraging the child's creativity at every turn, for they understand that it is through creative experiences that the child explores the possible avenues by which self-actualization may be achieved.

Self-actualization is not a purely intellectual process. The fulfillment of a child's potentialities also depends on whether the emotional equipment she/he develops has a generally facilitative or inhibitory effect on the unfolding of special talents. For this reason, it is also important for the creative teacher (and parent) to seize opportunities for helping the child to discover and understand herself/himself as a person. Self-understanding is not an all-or-nothing affair, for there can be various *degrees* of self-understanding, and it is not being unrealistic to expect average children to develop a modicum of understanding about the meaning of their emotional reactions and general behavior. For them to achieve this, however, they must have teachers and parents who are not only skillful in understanding and explaining human behavior but who possess a degree of self-understanding themselves.

Adequate fulfillment of the five basic needs is a minimal requirement for good mental health. The home has a very great responsibility in helping the child fulfill these needs. Some homes, however, do *not* fulfill these responsibilities as well as they should. Since the presence or absence of good mental health powerfully influences the child's learning in school, the school has a major stake in repairing damaged mental health and in enhancing good mental health.

MENTAL HEALTH AND CLASSROOM LEARNING

One of the typical reactions to lack of need-fulfillment in one or more areas is that of *anxiety*. Anxiety of the type considered here is not a simple fear reaction to a specific threatening situation; it is rather a chronic apprehensiveness about everything in general.

Behavior of Neurotically Anxious Children

The neurotically anxious child is afraid of life itself, meeting all experiences with the same combination of subjectively experienced uneasiness and apprehension. The anxiety often manifests itself in such signs as gastrointestinal disturbances, nervous mannerisms, sleep difficulties, heart palpitations, or other physical symptoms. As might be expected, such anxiety reactions become even more acute in those situations to which the child has become most sensitized by experiencing failure of need-fulfillment in similar or related situations. A child who does not feel secure in affectional relationships with parents, for instance, is likely to feel most acutely anxious when confronted with another authority figure, like the classroom teacher, who might again expose her/him to rejection.

Generalized neurotic anxiety in a child's life can be quite disabling in its influence on the child's learning and personal efficiency. No person has an unlimited amount of energy available, and the anxious child invests so much energy in confronting problems that there is little left over to conduct the ordinary affairs of life. In order to cope with anxiety, the anxious child is likely to make excessive use of

18

the various defense mechanisms—repression, rationalization, projection, reaction-formation, and the like. Since the excessive use of these mechanisms seldom settles issues, but only serves to avoid them or render them temporarily less acute, the whole effort is largely wasted and the child is soon back where she/he started, despite a great expenditure of effort.

A few children, for instance, react to anxiety by withdrawing from situations that are similar or even remotely related to the original need-frustrating situation. They may even carry it further than this by withdrawing from social relationships altogether. These children may seem to the classroom teacher to be among the most easily handled, but their solemn obedience and amenability only hide a deep inner turmoil. Other children may become quite aggressive and antisocial as a way of retaliating against a world that they feel has short-changed them. In this case, their rejection is likely to include, *or even focus on,* school learning as a symbol of adult-imposed requirements. Their retaliation may take the form of a zealous kind of troublemaking that leaves the teacher with a feeling of exasperation and hopelessness.

What the Teacher Can Do

The classroom teacher can regard anxiety and its behavioral correlates as one of the best general indicators of inadequate need-fulfillment and poor mental health. Such analysis, however, is not complete until one can identify the need-area which, through deprivation, resulted in that anxiety.

With experience, one may come to know that children who makes nuisances of themselves by "hanging around" before and after school, eager to help the teacher with each and every little task, may in fact be groping for a secure affectional relationship that they do not have at home. When a pupil displays "showoff" behavior, an understanding teacher's first response is not to react moralistically, but to consider the possibility that this *may* be the only way the child can achieve the least measure of self-esteem. If another pupil becomes unsettled whenever new or different materials or experiences are introduced, the wise teacher may ask where the child's safety and security needs have not been adequately met.

The effective classroom teacher also knows that deficiencies at home, though critical, can be at least partially compensated for in the classroom. To be sure, teachers attempt to prevent classroom experiences that might adversely affect the self-esteem of students; but they also try to utilize the unique capabilities of each student so that fulfillment of self-esteem needs is maximized for the entire classroom group. Where they observe a student suffering from lack of self-esteem, they do what they can to provide opportunities for the student to obtain *realistic* feelings of success, however small. Similarly, although teachers can hardly be expected to provide a completely effective antidote to a severe lack of strong affectional relationships in the home, they can provide examples of understanding, kindly, and acceptant authority figures, who have a genuine liking for students.

Finally, classroom teachers can have a very significant influence in their efforts to help each student achieve a unique pattern of self-actualization. By encouraging students to use their curricular and extracurricular experiences to discover and develop their own special abilities, every teacher can make a most important contribution to the future mental health of students.

EFFECT OF TEACHER'S MENTAL HEALTH ON PUPIL LEARNING

The manner in which classroom teachers characteristically fulfill their needs has implications not only for their own mental health but for the mental health of their students as well.

One of the most important generalizations that can be made about the mentally healthy, well-adjusted teacher is that such a person is free to be child-oriented and problem-oriented. We say "free" in this way because she/he is not laboring under the burden of personal problems which sap emotional strength and leave little time or energy for anything else. Such a teacher enjoys solving classroom problems because personal problems have not whipped her/him or even tried her/his patience. Feeling positive about learning and life, this teacher creates a desire for learning and an eagerness for life in the minds of students. For students who are struggling to achieve their own patterns of self-actualization, the confident teacher exemplifies the worth-while values that can result when self-actualization is truly attained.

HOW TO TEACH MENTAL HEALTH PRINCIPLES

A teacher's impact on pupils' mental health is exerted in a hundred incidents a day, in which attitudes and basic values about people are expressed. Probably few classroom teachers can or should take much time during the day to talk specifically about mental health as a separate topic, although a teacher can try to give children insight as they learn. On the other hand, no teacher can escape responsibility for the way her/his personal behavior affects pupils during the day. Thus, if a classroom teacher is to help pupils gain increasing emotional maturity, she/he must react to the events of each moment with appropriate emotionality. Genuine self-direction must be exemplified in the teacher's own behavior, or the pupils will not be able to see or understand what talk about emotional maturity means. Perhaps more important, they will not have a human model to emulate, with all the attractive power and incentive that a model provides. Certainly, a teacher cannot foster in pupils a positive respect for other people by treating any members of a class in a disrespectful or hostile manner. In short, in the area of mental health, as in so many other areas of teaching, one can teach no more than she/he personally understands and exemplifies.

The American school is not a center for therapy for severely maladjusted children. However, the school is the only organized institution in our society which has an opportunity to become acquainted with every child and to influence every child for a period of years. Therefore, there are a good many conscious and unconscious pressures on the school to take over a diagnostic, and even a therapeutic, function which schools were not originally designed to perform. As one mother siad, almost in caricature, "Well if you can't handle my son here in school, how do you expect me to do anything with him at home?

Nonetheless, entirely within its traditional purposes and methods, the school is perhaps the one great potential source of help for millions of young Americans in the following ways:

1. A classroom teacher is in a better prepared position than many parents to help the child learn to *think* in an organized, objective fashion. In many cases, more than the average adult, the teacher is inclined to tackle problems in a clear, realistic fashion because of personal inclinations and because of years of training in just this approach.

2. For a great many children, the school provides the only planned, continuous experience in learning to set, and go after, goals. Goal setting is a specific skill and involves attitudes about oneself and the world which require a great deal of practice to perfect.

3. The school, and only the school, is in a position to teach all children the basic facts and principles which account for human behavior. Although it is true that we would like to know a great deal more than we now know in this field, there is enough knowledge to help anyone make sense out of his own and others' behavior.

4. Learning facts about human behavior does not necessarily make anyone—child or adult—more able to be objectively self-appraising and self-understanding. In addition to knowledge, it requires that the person be *willing* to look at himself. A classroom teacher who treats children in a friendly, emotionally supportive manner can foster such a willingness, along with giving them the necessary knowledge.

5. Out of the same context can come an attitude of *wanting* to understand other people rather than just blindly reacting to what they do. To understand people requires the highest order of intellectual skill. It requires a great deal of factual information, a great deal of practical, disciplined imagination, and a great deal of practice in making interpretations and checking their accuracy.

If it is worth teaching mathematical reasoning from the primary grades onward, it would not seem too much to start teaching children to reason about human behavior, in simple ways at first, no later than the intermediate grades. Several trial programs of this kind have been carried out experimentally at the elementary school level, but much more work waits to be done.

Anxiety: A Deterrent to Effective Learning

by Frederick F. Lighthall

The tendency to stop and think and the tendency to stop thinking both hold close relationships to the goals of education on the one hand and, on the other, to children's perceptions of danger and their experiences of anxiety. Neither danger nor anxiety is confined to the rare or the pathological. Quite the contrary; they intrude regularly into our own and our students' interests, work, and thoughts.

To understand anxiety, as psychologists view it, is not a simple task. The essential difficulty lies in the fact that anxiety operates only when something very crucial to the anxious person is *absent* from his conscious thoughts. To understand anxiety it is necessary to understand how something which was extremely important to an individual has come to be purposefully pushed from the person's conscious memory and so slyly pushed that she/he is completely unaware of the pushing. Without this understanding, behavior actually generated by anxiety is interpreted incorrectly as being in response to events in the immediate environment and judged to be "silly," "queer," "stupid," or "crazy."

THE ANXIETY EXPERIENCE ANALYZED

Perhaps the best way to begin to learn about anxiety is to get a vivid impression of it as it is experienced. The reader is urged to read carefully the narrative description of an anxiety experience given in this section.

The experience was described by a successful graduate student conducting observations in classrooms as a part of training in educational psychology. (The proper names used are not real and serve only to distinguish early experiences from later ones.)

> I was going over [to the Abbott School] twice a week; the first couple of times I was going over it was interesting. I felt I was learning a lot . . . Then I found, after two or three times, that I was finding it more and more difficult to go over there. . . .I was tense during the time, . . . terribly self-conscious. . . . When I left I felt . . . you know . . . a great feeling of relief . . . Like often as you walk out of a party where you've been "trying to say the right thing" you get this feeling of relaxation.
>
> And then I found that it was harder and harder to go there, that I woke up tired, that the previous evening it was hard for me to

do any studying . . . I was tired getting up in the morning. . . . Sometimes you can wake up and you can just move from there, and other times it takes you a long time to get going. And this was a long time getting going. It wasn't that I was *feeling* sick but I felt that if I wanted to I could have felt sick—that if I were to let myself I could have gotten headaches or . . . you know . . . if I were sick, felt that one should really stay in bed.

. . . .

. . . And finally for two weeks I didn't go. . . . the first week I rationalized it and said well, hell, I got a lot of work to do, and so on. The second week I realized . . . well, sit down and figure this out because you can't really go if you feel this way.

This description of what we shall call the *anxiety experience* contains four parts. One is the *anxiety cue:* the particular thought, memory, or sensation which precipitates the second part, the *anxiety affect.* The anxiety affect is a surge of emotion, somewhat like that experienced in fear, which is unpleasant and demands relief. This affective response is a reaction to the cue and, whether mild or severe, sets off changes in the nervous system and viscera which have reverberations thoughout the body. A third part of the anxiety experience—we shall call it the *primary anxiety reaction*—is a defensive or withdrawing move by the anxious person. The primary reaction may take many forms, at once or serially—physical escape from the immediate situation or diversionary activity, thoughts, or feelings. A fourth part is what might be called the *adaptive anxiety reaction.* It is very different from the other three parts—it occurs much less frequently and requires either a fundamentally confident self-concept or considerable courage to face fear. It probably also requires more abstract intelligence. The adaptive reaction consists essentially in the individual's posing the question, "Why am I feeling this way?" and in seeking an answer by analyzing the conditions surrounding the onset and cessation of the anxiety affect.

For the graduate student, the anxiety affect appeared in the form of tenseness and self-consciousness. We may surmise from the account given that the cue was something in the school; the affect appeared in school or at the thought of the classroom and disappeared, with relief, when he left school. The primary reaction appeared in the form of awareness of fatigue, slowness in "getting going" in the morning, and heightened awareness of bodily aches and pains. The adaptive reaction was his realization that something was wrong, and his pursuit, to which we will turn later, of what was behind the experience.

UNCOVERING THE ANXIETY CUE

In considering the cue lying behind the graduate student's anxiety affect, note the means whereby he "discovers" the cue.

> The second week I realized . . . well, sit down and figure this out because you can't really go if you feel this way. And then I got to thinking that the grades I was sitting in [at Abbott] were from the second grade through the . . . seventh . . . And that paralleling these years when I went to school in . . . [Bakertown] which was a lousy school, where I didn't have anything in common with the other kids . . . I hated the school, I hated the teachers, I cut class. . . . I didn't do well academically. Before then, the first, second, third grades I was doing real well; . . . and then I wasn't doing well. . . . I had no happy experiences while being *in* school. The things that come to mind are that I didn't do my homework . . . I was always poor in spelling . . . and always being chastised by the teachers 'cause I *should* do well. . . . you should do well and you're not doing well . . . so I wasn't . . . I was having trouble with the teacher. I was having trouble with the *kids*. Because I didn't like to fight, and of course this is the sort of situation where you find yourself . . . where everyone wants you to fight . . . And also I tend to be stubborn enough . . . which meant that I got up *their* anger but yet wouldn't fight that much . . . So school wasn't fun from either the kids' or the teachers' standpoint.

> The only thing that happened was that I got advanced a grade in a subject. I stayed in the fourth grade and went up to the fifth grade for social studies 'cause I was specially good in that. And I came to find this alienated me even more with the fourth graders; and the fifth graders didn't accept me. And I kind of felt between two worlds. And this was the time when I would cut class . . . I'd cut *school.* I'd feel sick in the morning, and then suddenly-get-well-at-nine-oh-five kind of idea.

> So anyway, the feeling I had was that what I was doing at [Abbott] was experiencing again going through the school at [Bakertown] . . . that the sort of kids there remind me of [Bakertown], the teacher's comments reminded me of teachers' comments . . . and it would set it off. . . .

> After I had . . . thought through the parallels between [Abbott] and [Bakertown], I could go back to [Abbott] and sit in a class. And although it wasn't easy, it was possible where before it

really wasn't possible. And not only could I sit in it and see things, but now I was able to draw parallels *in* class that I hadn't been able to before . . . and therefore able to understand the situation.

What conditions were necessary for the student to re-awaken buried memories of his own school days? First, he had to notice and attend consciously to his anxiety affect. Second, he had to possess the knowledge (a) that feelings do not just arise spontaneously, but come from somewhere and are responsive to something; (b) that there was a connection between his own feelings while observing and his sluggishness and hints of illness in anticipation of going to Abbott (i.e., a connection between anxiety affect and primary anxiety re-action); and (c) that there was an important connection be-tween, on the one hand, any childhood memories which might "spontaneously" occur while in or thinking about the classroom at Abbott and, on the other, his feelings about being in the Abbott classroom. A third condition for recover-ing memories about the cue was that the graduate student feel confident that thinking about such connections promised gains that outweighed the unpleasantness avoided by not thinking about them.

THE NATURE AND IMPORTANCE OF DANGER

The term "danger" refers to a complicated *relationship* between person and environment. Danger is a psychological, not physical, concept: it arises from a subjective judgment. This judgment consists in a person's weighing of two sets of forces—the *demands seen* in the present situation and the personal *resources* with which she/he can meet demands.

There appear to be two basic modes of reacting to danger. One is to approach it with the aim of eventual com-prehension and mastery. The other is to avoid it with the aim of immediate comfort. Most of us vacillate back and forth between these two problem-solving strategies. Some of us are more cautious; others, more adventurous. Whatever our pre-dispostions, they are rooted in our experience of success or failure in attempts to understand and master.

It sometimes happens that we are caught in a relatively brief situation in which events are unexpected and incom-prehensible to us, or in which we think they promise harm. We usually try both modes of neutralizing danger—approach for understanding and mastery if we cannot escape, and escape if we cannot understand or master. If both attempts fail and our diagnosis of danger does not change, we experience a flood of frightful and desparate emotion properly called terror. Or, if the danger is recurrent rather than brief, and if we can neither master nor avoid its recurrence, we experience crescendos of apprehension in our forced contacts with it. These crescendos drop sharply after the situation has become safe once more.

What do we mean by inescapable and unmasterable danger? Quite simply, we mean helplessness.

The graduate student was afraid of fighting in a group where fighting was frequent and important. Furthermore, he was placed in a school situation in social studies which caused estrangement between him and his peers. He was powerless to change or escape from this estrangement.

FUNCTIONS OF PURPOSEFUL FORGETTING

After the experience of helplessness has passed, there are two typical modes of dealing with the memory of it. These modes are exactly parallel to the two modes of dealing with danger. The *approach* tendency seeks to hold the memory in mind, to consider it, and to try to understand what happened, why it was unexpected, how it might have been prevented, and how it may be avoided or mastered in the future. The *avoidance* tendency consciously resists attending to the memory. All of us at one time or another have said to ourselves, "Well, don't get yourself upset over *that* again! After all, it's over." Also, we frequently find it helpful, in putting something out of mind, to divert our attention to problems in the present—especially soluble problems.

The process of purposefully forgetting becomes more and more habitual where the danger has been unavoidable and beyond mastery. A transformation gradually takes place, as with all habits. First, the tendency to stop thinking of the unpleasant danger becomes anticipatory. That is, at the slightest suggestion of a reminder of the danger, diversionary thoughts are attended to. Second, the anticipatory memory avoidance becomes so habitual that it no longer demands the slightest attention. That is, the process of memory avoiding itself becomes unconscious. In this respect suppression is like walking, driving an automobile, knitting, or any other activity with repetitive components: it becomes so fluent that we can attend to other things while doing it. When suppression becomes habitual to this extent it is referred to as *repression.*

FEAR AND ANXIETY HAVE DIFFERENT CONSEQUENCES

A distinction between fear and anxiety is now possible. Fear consists essentially in an apprehensive reaction to something perceived in the environment which has been linked with previously experienced pain, bewilderment, or humiliation. Fear is a reaction to a *recognized* sign of harm. The experience of anxiety is similar but contains an essential ingredient missing in fear—repression. The graduate student was not afraid of Abbott classrooms. The sign of harm which acts as the anxiety cue is no longer consciously recognized as being linked to a dangerous situation. Abundant evidence shows, however, that in anxiety an important kind of recognition takes place below awareness. It is this below-awareness sensing of the anxiety cue as being linked to danger that sets off the anxiety affect.

One of the tragic consequences of repression is that it deprives the person of the opportunity to bring her/his growing powers of understanding and mastery to bear on the danger. In fear, that opportunity is at least initially present. The feared object or situation can be talked about and openly considered, thus affording opportunity for reassessment of its demands or of personal resources in relation to its mastery.

ANXIETY AROUSED BY RELATED SITUATIONS

Consider one final but extremely important characteristic of anxiety: the tendency for anxiety affect to be cued off in more and more different situations. We shall call this tendency *anxiety generalization.*

Anxiety generalization occurs when the anxious person begins to experience anxiety affect not merely in the presence of the original anxiety cue, but also at the occurrence of related situations.

Generalization is facilitated when two similar but not identical situations produce helplessness. For example, one of the most frequent and unavoidable situations in which children experience both helplessness and associated humiliation is produced in a variety of school situations. It is the test. The test takes many forms and occurs in a wide variety of school contexts. Repeated feelings of helplessness in tests are undoubtedly handled by children in ways that lead to anxiety. That is, they attempt to avoid tests and to avoid thinking about past tests. As a result the possibility of attending to the specific weaknesses shown by the test and to ways in which the weakness might be remedied is removed. Test anxiety undoubtedly generalizes to evaluation in general, and probably in many cases to situations where the most important fact to the child is that there is a person in authority who has the power to find out, even if she/he doesn't use the power.

IMPLICATIONS FOR EDUCATION

What does the nature of anxiety imply for educational goals and practice? In the first place, it should be clear by now that anxiety is not simply the feeling of unpleasant emotion. Some of the most essential components of anxiety are closely tied up with educational goals. Specifically what does our understanding of the nature and development of anxiety imply for classroom perception and action?

The teacher who is able to perceive the student's sense of helplessness will be a force in the prevention of anxiety and in the facilitation of mastery. What are some of the signs of helpless feelings in students?

1. Hostility consistently expressed toward the subject matter: "Aw, do we have to do this lousy stuff?" The nature of the student's problem will not be clear, but that there is a problem that the student does not feel up to coping with will be clear.

2. Consistent bewilderment or *blocking* in spite of several explanations: "I just don't get it. I can't get *any* of that stuff." In the upper grades and in high school, bewilderment will be shown more in the absence of participation, absence of attention, and absence of completed or attempted homework.

3. Ready promises followed by procrastination and "forgetting."

4. Dependency on the teacher and/or other students for answers to questions which the student herself/himself could answer with but slight thought or independent search.

Some of these signs may not indicate anxiety affect or anxiety reactions directly, but rather may reflect a discrepancy between the curriculum content and competing demands which appear more real to the student. Where the discrepancy exists, it creates a conflict which sometimes places too great a burden on the student's capacity to attend to classroom events—she/he is pulled in two important directions while sitting in the classroom. Here, too, if conflicting demands continue, the student is likely to develop a sense of helplessness and will tend to give attention to the more immediate, tangible, and persistent demands. Other demands, such as assignments or concepts whose significance has escaped her/him, are frequently pushed from memory. For students who resolve the conflict in this way, school and school-like demands and activities become an occasion for anxiety.

WHAT THE TEACHER CAN DO

One of the best strategies for the teacher who is aware of a discrepancy between curricular specifications and the life demands of the students is to reach out and re-establish contact with them and to capitalize on the contact. It takes two steps which go on continuously, each feeding the other. *First,* by stimulating group discussion or the writing of autobiographies and accounts of critical incidents in family life, growing up, moving to new neighborhoods, and the like, the teacher assesses the main directions of competing attention and specific school disatisfactions of the students. *Second,* the teacher uses the situations of conflict and competition in constructing reading and writing activities and in selecting from the required curriculum those parts which would appeal to the motivations and issues of concern contained in the discussions and themes.

When the elements common to both curricular objectives and the concerns and underlying motives of the student are found and used, the helplessness students feel when confronted with insistent demands in their own lives and the demands of a less meaningful school curriculum can be largely removed.

An essential part of helplessness is the control of the standard of quantity and quality of work by another person. As adults, we have control over the selection of standards under which we will work. If present or prospective employment standards are too demanding, we have control over our movement to another situation. Children in school, however, have no such control unless the teacher makes provision for it. If the teacher does not make provision for a sliding scale of either quantity or quality, then a uniform standard of work is employed. Such a standard renders those who work below it helpless in important respects.

Any teaching strategy which enables the student to control her/his own pace in approaching school tasks will to that extent render unnecessary any recourse to defensive avoidance of the task. While it is usually (even in college) too much to ask a student completely to control her/his own learning, an important sense of autonomous competence will be gained if an opportunity is given for self-pacing.

One good way to provide for differences in students' control over pace is to offer and emphasize principal assignments and then suggest an array of specific tasks which can either serve as additional credit or, in certain numbers or combinations, substitute for the main assignment entirely. This needs planning and may create some extra work in evaluation, but it can engender positive involvement with work and better quality. It allows some students who feel they have to strike off in individual paths and others who do not like to be *told* what to do to approach an educative task, to avoid something distasteful, and to develop a sense of selectivity and control over the forces acting on them.

EFFECTS OF ANXIETY ON SCHOOL EXPERIENCE

We have been considering the effect of school experience on the development of anxiety or, more optimistically, on the development of the tendency to approach school tasks with the hope of understanding and mastery. Now let us turn briefly to the effects of anxiety on school experience.

Anxiety, self-concept, and the ability to engage in deliberate thinking are closely interrelated. Children in school constantly face situations whose demands they must compare with their own resources. Whenever a student's assessment of situational demands leads her/him to conclude that they are greater than her/his resources, that student faces a dangerous situation—one in which she/he feels the promise of humiliation is great enough to call for escape.

Most children in most classrooms grow steadily in their power to cope with classroom danger. In any event, the humiliation which comes from classroom failure is usually short-lived. Some children experience their failures more intensely than others, however. Also, some children come to school having experienced greater failure at home than others. Some teachers are more punitive, some classroom groups more humiliating, than others. Whatever the case, it seems safe to say that all children have experienced humiliation in failure severe enough to be wary of its possible recurrence.

For those children who are especially wary and sensitive to the danger in situations they face, the innocent classroom discussion question can be unpleasant and can come to cue off anxiety affect. For these children a vicious circle becomes established: the teacher puts a question, anxiety affect is cued off, the child worries about the other children's and the teacher's reactions to possible failure, those worry-thoughts take the place of thought about the question and its answer, the first plausible answer that is hit upon is seized as a way out of the worry and danger, and this first answer is expressed. Frequently the answer has only limited relevance to the question, because the child has hurriedly interpreted it. When the question has been interpreted correctly, the answer is frequently of less than the expected quality, even for the child concerned. As a result the child becomes aware of a relatively poor personal performance, and her/his apprehensions about questions and her/his ability to answer them are "proven" to be realistic.

If one of the purposes of schooling is to help children carefully to consider questions and answers in search of the best of several possible interpretations and answers, then children's anxiety or predisposition to worry about failure when faced with questions is a hindrance. Experimental evidence has shown that threats to self-esteem, such as censure or invidious comparisons, increase the tendency to arrive at quick conclusions. Evidence also shows that persons whose self-image—the one they carry around with them, so to speak—is low also tend to arrive at premature judgments. When a person with chronic low self-esteem is placed in a threatening situation, her/his judgments are most impulsive of all.

The teacher who wants to build up the habit of deliberation should realize that for children who feel questions they cannot answer are dangerous, deliberation merely prolongs their contact with the unanswered question and increases anxiety affect. The advice, "Now wait! Stop and think about it for a second," is not enough. The student has to feel that this kind of pause will not be interpreted by the teacher or the peer group as stupidity. The teacher who has set students at ease on this point will have helped the anxious child as well as those with sturdier self-concepts. To create an atmosphere in which exploratory, tentative thought can be engaged in comfortably is difficult. It is impossible to do so if the teacher feels she/he has to "cover the material" first and worry about the atmosphere afterward. Covering material creates its own atmosphere—and it is neither tentative nor deliberate!

A teacher who is comfortable in saying, "I don't know. How would we find out?" when faced with a student's question that cannot be readily answered is a teacher whose actions tell the students that it is all right not to know *and* that it is possible, and all right, not even to know the way to find the answer. The teacher who poses questions with the intention of eliciting thought about, rather than answers to, the questions is providing students with an image of what it is like to deliberate. She/he is giving instruction in deliberation, not by talking about it, but by engaging in it.

Finally, the teacher who examines *out loud* the questions which she/he puts to students is providing a model for interpreting questions which will help the anxious and the impulsive student. If teachers encourage each student to examine a question as part of her/his answer they will be going even further in helping the student learn to think.

Motivation: An Initiation to the Learning Process

by Don E. Hamachek

Motivation, for the purposes of this article, is a *process*. That is, it is a process that can (a) lead students into experiences in which learning can occur; (b) energize and activate students and keep them reasonably alert; (c) keep their attention focused in one direction at a time. We must admit at the outset that there is no one formula, or strategy, or set of devices which will motivate all pupils in the same way or the same degree. Rather, we must understand that what turns some students on is the very thing that may turn others off; that what motivates John may discourage Bill; that what excites Mary may bore Sally. Furthermore, the same individual may be motivated by different factors at different times.

When students are motivated, they are usually energized and directed toward rather selective behavior. If we view motivation from the point of view of the behaver, we must say that she/he is *never* unmotivated. That is to say, each of us, no matter who she/he is or what she/he does, is motivated by a continuous endeavor to maintain and enhance personal adequacy. If a pupil does well in school, she/he is more likely to be energized and directed toward selecting school-related activities than is a pupil who does poorly in school. Like anyone else, students do not long stay motivated by things in which they experience more failure than success.

SELF-CONCEPT AS RELATED TO MOTIVATION AND LEARNING

As William James put it, "The Self is the sum total of all that a person can call his." More than that, it is a person's awareness of individual existence in terms of all of her/his beliefs, attitudes, and opinions.

Increasing evidence indicates that student failures in basic school subjects—as well as the misguided motivation and lack of academic involvement characteristic of the underachiever, the dropout, the culturally disadvantaged, and the failure—may be due in part to unhealthy perceptions of the self and the world. Many students, for example, have difficulty in school, not because of low intelligence or poor eyesight, but because they have learned to consider themselves unable to do academic work.

There is evidence to suggest that the way students feel about themselves and their ability to do schoolwork is positively related to what they think others expect of them. For example, students with low academic self-concepts are likely to perceive parents and teachers as having low expectations for them. That is, they perceive others as having little faith in their (the students') ability to do well in school in the first place. Experiments in behavioral research have shown that the experimenter's *expectations* for subjects' performances can be significant determinants of how the subjects actually respond.

Just as children *learn* to walk and *learn* to talk, they *learn* about themselves. We learn who we are and what we are from the ways in which we were treated while growing up, not to mention how we are treated on a daily basis by those around us. This is what the psychiatrist Harry Stack Sullivan called "learning about the self from the mirror of other people." Like each of us, our students learn to view themselves as liked, acceptable, and capable from *having been* liked and accepted, and from *having been* successful. The crucial key to increasing the proportion of students with adequate self-concepts, with adequate feelings of self-esteem, is to help students toward success experiences that teach them they are worthwhile people.

TEACHER VARIABLES RELATED TO MOTIVATION AND LEARNING

Teacher Personality

We would probably all agree that it is quite possible for two teachers of equal intelligence, training, and grasp of subject matter to differ in the extent to which they are able to encourage student motivation and learning. Part of the difference can be accounted for by the effect of a teacher's personality on the learners.

Examining desirable personal characteristics of teachers as these characteristics are identified by students, we find for the most part, these charicteristics group themselves under the general headings of capacity for warmth, patience, tolerance, and interest in students. What happens when these personal qualities are related to the more rigid test of whether having them makes any difference in the actual performance of students?

One investigation, for example, found that there are positive relationships between the extent to which a teacher shows a personal interest in and willingness to listen to students' ideas and the creativity shown by students. Another study found that warm and considerate teachers got an unusual amount of original poetry and art from their high school students. It has also been found that teachers with a greater capacity for warmth favorably affected their pupils' interests in science. In still another study, student learning was related to interaction between different teacher and student personalities. Comparisons were made between various teacher-pupil personality combinations in terms of pupil achievement, teacher knowledge, and classroom settings. It was found that the well-integrated (healthy, well-rounded, flexible) teachers were most effective with *all* types of students. Two other identified teacher personality "types" (fearful and turbulent) were successful with only certain types of students.

Teacher Interaction Styles

Even though there is not one *best* way to interact with students, research has shown that some ways are better than others.

For example, Flanders studied teacher influence styles, pupil attitudes, and resulting achievement in seventh-grade social studies and eighth-grade mathematics. He uncovered four essential elements of teacher influence in the classrooms in which motivation, learning, and attitudes were superior.

1. The teacher was able to provide spontaneously a range of roles that varied from fairly active, dominative supervision to a more reflective, discriminating support.
2. The teacher was able to switch roles at will rather than pursue a single interaction style to the exclusion of other possibilities.
3. The teacher was able to bridge the gap between the diagnosis of a given situation and the course of action she/he should take.
4. The teacher was able to combine sensitivity and critical awareness so that, as the classroom's master observer, she/he was able to make reasonable diagnoses of current conditions.

Interestingly, those teachers who were *not* successful were those who were inclined to use the same instructional procedures and interaction styles in a more or less rigid fashion. That is, there seemed to be little variation from one classroom day or situation to the next.

In an earlier study, detailed stenographic records, observation charts, and various time charts were kept on 47 teachers of social studies in high school ranked as superior and 47 ranked well below average in teaching skills. Practically every conceivable act and every expression of teacher and pupil interaction were considered—about 37 factors in all. The following are fragmentary interaction expressions which distinguished good from poor teachers.

Characteristic Comments Made by Poor But Not by Good Teachers

Are you working hard? . . . Aren't you ever going to learn that work? . . . Everyone sit up straight, please. . . . I'm afraid you're confused. . . . No, that's wrong. . . . Oh dear, don't you know that? . . . Oh, sit down. . . . Say something. [Nearly one hundred different expressions were listed. Note the overtones of frustration, futility, and impatience which sound through most.]

Characteristic Comments Made by Good But Not by Poor Teachers

Aha, that's a new idea. . . . Are you going to accept that as an answer? I should like more proof. . . . Do you suppose you could supply a better word? . . . Can you prove your statement? . . . Don't you really think you could? . . . I'm not quite clear on that—think a moment. . . . Let's stick to the question. . . . Probably my last question wasn't a good one. [There was a long list of such expressions. Note the emphasis on challenging the student, on pushing and encouraging her/him to go beyond where she/he may be at the moment.]

There is also evidence that when a teacher is able to personalize her/his interaction she/he is apt to be more successful, particularly in motivating students to do better work. It certainly does seem to be true that teachers who show an active personal interest in their students' progress are likely to be more successful motivators than teachers who are inclined to be distant and impersonal.

Summary Statement

We must remember that in comprehensive studies, there is much overlap between the personal characteristics and teaching styles of "high" and "low" motivator teachers. None of the research demonstrates that there are classroom practices which are used exclusively by either kind of teacher. Nevertheless, there are characteristics which seem to appear more consistently in one group than the other. For example, when it comes to classroom behavior, interaction patterns, and teaching styles, teachers who are superior in encouraging motivation and learning in students seem to exhibit more of the following characteristics:

1. Willingness to be flexible, to be direct or indirect as the situation demands
2. Capacity to perceive the world from the student's point of view
3. Ability to "personalize" their teaching
4. Willingness to experiment, to try out new things
5. Skill in asking questions (as opposed to seeing self as a kind of answering service)
6. Knowledge of subject matter and related areas
7. Skill in establishing definite examination procedures
8. Willingness to provide definite study helps
9. Capacity to reflect an appreciative attitude (evidenced by nods, comments, smiles, etc.)
10. Conversational manner in teaching—informal, easy style

STUDENT VARIABLES RELATED TO MOTIVATION AND LEARNING

We talk a great deal about individual differences in learning ability among students, but we must remember that there are also differences in student personality characteristics which apparently interact with teaching and motivation. Let us turn now to a discussion of those student variables which seem most related to motivation and learning.

Student Personality

Three separate experiments have reported findings which indicate that teaching methods do, indeed, interact with student personality characteristics to affect motivation and learning. In all of these experiments some students were placed in discussion or lecture sections where expectations were clearly defined, while other students were placed in more open-ended sections where they were free to establish objectives and course procedures. A certain kind of student emerged who appeared to require a high degree of structure to make optimum progress. These students were described as being personally insecure and dependent. On the other hand, there were the more personally secure students who found the permissive, open-ended class very much to their liking and who flourished under its conditions. In any case, whether a student is secure or insecure, dependent or independent, these personality dimensions do make a difference when it comes to determining whether one teaching method or another will be successful as a motivating technique.

Compulsiveness and anxiety are two other student personality characteristics which apparently influence motivation and learning. For example, it has been found that when teaching is structured, compulsive children do substantially better than less compulsive children. Highly anxious children do poorly in unstructured classrooms. Children who are both highly anxious and highly compulsive do their best work in structured classes.

Other evidence also points to individual differences in personality factors. It has been found that some pupils are more concerned about feelings and personal relationships, while others are mainly achievement-oriented. Classes made up mostly of students of the first type tend to accept the teacher whom they like and reject the teacher whom they dislike on personal grounds. Classes composed of students of the second type pay less attention to teacher warmth in estimating their acceptance or rejection of certain teachers.

Student Reactions To Praise and Blame

Generally speaking, praise is a more powerful motivator than either blame or reproof of the work performance of students. The effects of praise and criticism on motivation and learning, however, are not so simple. Several studies have indicated that the effects of praise or blame were related to personality differences. The major conclusions reached by these studies indicate that—

1. When introverts and extroverts are grouped together (as is the case in most classrooms), either praise or blame is more effective in increasing the work output of fifth-grade pupils than no external incentives.
2. If repeated often enough, praise increases the work output of introverts until it is significantly higher than that of introverts who are blamed or extroverts who are praised.
3. If repreated often enough, blame increases the work output of extroverts until it is significantly higher than that of extroverts who are praised or introverts who are blamed.

It is apparent that the use of praise or blame has different effects on children with different personality characteristics. It seems altogether possible that indiscriminate praise may be as detrimental to student's motivation and learning as indiscriminate blame or criticism. Perhaps one way to enhance our teaching effectiveness is to be constantly sensitive to personality differences among students in order to use incentives such as praise and blame wisely and appropriately.

Student Reactions to Success and Failure

We probably do not have to go much further than our own life experiences in order to understand the differential effects of success and failure. What is a success experience for one student is a failure experience for another.

Although each of our levels of aspiration determines to a large extent what we interpret as failure or success, another factor worth considering is our history of successes and failures. For example, to fail at something is more tolerable if we have had a history of success in that particular endeavor.

In a sense each of us, like each of our students, has what we could call a "psychological bank account." Just as we deposit money in our savings account, we deposit successes in our psychological account. Some people have less money, therefore can deposit less and, in fact, have less to draw on in time of need. Somewhat the same is true of success. Some adults and children simply have fewer successes to deposit in their psychological accounts, and just as it is possible to go financially bankrupt, it is possible to experience *psychological* bankruptcy. The difference is that when we are financially bankrupt, there is always the possibility of starting over again. Not so with psychological bankruptcy—one's failures are not so easily wiped away. If we take this analogy into the school world, we can all think of students we know who pay their way through school (if they make it) on what amounts to a "psychological deficit financing plan." For the most part, they are students for whom school success is neither easily won nor easily available. Just as having enough money encourages some to invest to make more, so having enough success encourages some to invest in greater success. But there has to be an "account" to begin with.

Research has shown that a person's success experiences contribute to her/his setting realistic levels of aspiration. People who have little money will sometimes engage in wild, risk-taking ventures to get more or become uncommonly conservative in order to reduce the risk of losing what they have. Students with histories of academic failure do somewhat the same thing. They set goals either so low that no hazard is involved or so high that success is impossible. They are, to a large extent, unpredictable. If we are to help these kinds of students be more consistent and more realistic about goal-setting, we ought to keep reminding ourselves that not all students will be motivated in the same way or interested in the same things. If we can remain aware of this, perhaps we can work harder at making success more available in more different ways and at more different levels. One way of doing this is to recognize that different students learn in different ways.

Student Differences in Learning Style

Although little formal research on this subject has been conducted, we are beginning to understand that there are, indeed, different "styles" for learning. There is no evidence that any one style is better or worse than another; if we are not careful, we may get caught in the trap of judging a learning style wrong just because it doesn't match our own. Most learning styles may be categorized as principally visual (reading), aural (listening), or physical (doing things), although it is possible that any one person may use more than one.

In the interests of effective motivation, it is important to identify each student's learning style as quickly as possible. If, for example, some students seem to learn best by reading, you may want not only to suggest books to them, but also to call on them more often in class to encourage them to experience more physical or verbal learning encounters. On the other hand, you may find it beneficial to encourage the more physical and aural students to read more. The point is that once we identify and become aware of each student's particular style for learning, we can encourage her/his best use of that style and help her/him experience other modes of learning as well.

TEACHING TECHNIQUES TO ENHANCE MOTIVATION AND LEARNING

We began by suggesting that there is no one best formula, or technique, which will motivate all students in the same way or to the same degree. As you have seen, the inter-action of self-concept, teacher, and student variables is so complex that no single approach can work by itself. What follows are some classroom techniques and procedures which may be of value to you in your day-to-day teaching.

Distribution of Practice and Rest in Learning

New learning material, like medicine, may be presented in large or small doses. It may be concentrated into relatively long unbroken periods of work or spread over several short sessions. Almost without exception, research concerned with the relative effectiveness of spacing new learning, whether motor or verbal, over a period of time and cramming it into a shorter time span shows that learning should be spaced in order to encourage and sustain high motivation.

How long should the intervals between learnings periods be? Within limits, longer learning periods call for longer rest periods. Generally speaking, new tasks should be introduced to students in small quantities with short initial learning sessions and short rest intervals. Gradual lengthening of the learning periods should follow. Also, to encourage a peak performance—on an exam, for example—concentrated practice of review the day before of well-learned material is usually desirable.

Knowledge of Results

A good technique for keeping students motivated is to provide them with essential information regarding their performance. Immediate, meaningful, specific knowledge of results, besides providing the information requisite to improvement of performance, has the advantage that awareness of progress serves as an incentive toward increased effort. Still more important, knowing what one doesn't know permits more effective distribution of one's time during study and/or practice sessions, because time isn't wasted rehearsing what is already known and is more likely to be allocated to what is not known.

The principle we are talking about can be simply stated: We are more likely to avoid mistakes if we know what our mistakes are in the first place. Hence, it is important to students that we indicate to them not only *what* was wrong but *why*.

Recitation During Learning

It has been reliably shown that reading combined with recitation is superior to reading alone for learning either concrete or abstract material. Reading a book is one thing, but remembering what was read is quite another. A valuable suggestion you might make to your students is that they either write out or recite in their own words the ideas or information in the new material they are learning. Another variation of the recitation idea is to encourage students to make up their own exams from the material they are reading and then try to answer their own questions. A good way to do this is to use the subheadings within each text as question guides. A great advantage of this self-testing system is that you find out immediately what you do not know and can take whatever remedial steps are appropriate.

Whole and Part Learning

Whole learning involves looking at the "big picture" first, before moving to the specifics. Part learning is just the reverse of this—each "part" or specific is studied in an effort to understand the total picture. Each system has its advantages, and wise teachers can assist their students to greater motivation and learning through the appropriate use of the whole and part methods.

The whole method of learning is probably better when—

- One wants a global picture of something without paying particular attention to details.
- One has an above-average IQ.
- The material is meaningful and more concrete than abstract.
- The material is closely knit together, on one theme, and not too long.

The part method of learning is better when—

- A student is not very capable intellectually. For example, slow learners and many disadvantaged students need to learn new material a step at a time because of the intellectual difficulty they may have in seeing the "whole" picture. Students need the reward and encouragement they can receive more frequently when learning smaller subunits of material.
- The material is long, complicated, and lacking a central theme running through it.

As you can see, the *character of the material* has much to do with the relative advantages of these two methods. For best motivational and learning results, a combination of the two methods is probably the best idea. For example, whatever you teach, it would be good practice to begin by helping your students see the "whole" picture. Then divide the whole picture into suitable subsections and approach it by the part method. Finally, review the whole to secure adequate organization of the parts into a total associative train.

Divergent Versus Convergent Questions

Sometimes, in our quest for "the right answers," we fall into the trap of asking only one kind of question—the convergent kind. Of course, there can be only one kind of answer to this sort of question, and it is usually a response which sorts through, synthesizes, and integrates answers from existing data. Divergent questions, however, invite a quite different type of thinking and responding. They demand answers which are original, novel, and creative. To ask a divergent question is to ask not only "What do you *know* about this?" but also "What do you *think* about this?" Convergent, memory-type questions do have a place in the classroom, but we may seriously hinder motivation and learning if we encourage only convergent thinking.

Exploiting the Motivational Possibilities of the Curriculum

Nearly everything in a curriculum is charged with psychological and motivational possibilities when looked at in terms of what it might do to help students find themselves, realize their potentialities, use their resources in productive ways, and enter into relationships which have a bearing on their ideas about school and attitudes toward themselves.

Sometimes, in our anxiety to cover a certain unit of material in a given amount of time, to give our students what we consider to be crucial information and knowledge, we end up teaching in a non-self-related manner. Many times students dislike English, or history, or social studies, or some other subject because it seems to have no personal meaning or relevance to their own lives. Indeed, many students see little relationship between what happens in school and what goes on outside of school. Can we make school more personally meaningful? Very probably so if we exploit the psychological as well as the academic content of a curriculum.

Exploiting the psychological possibilities of a curriculum offers exciting new avenues for enhancing motivation and learning. This doesn't mean that we negate the importance of content—not at all. In fact, our concern about how to motivate students may be less of a problem if we can teach in a more self-related rather than a less self-related manner. In the final analysis, none of us is highly motivated to learn about those things which appear to be disengaged from and unconnected to our own personal lives.

Creativity: An Extension of the Learning Parameters

by E. Paul Torrance

The demands of the times have fostered among educators in all fields and at all levels an unprecedented interest in creativity. The urgent demands of the moment are reinforced by several quite legitimate concerns of long standing among educators. These persistent and recurrent legitimate concerns include such educational goals as the production of fully functioning, mentally healthy, well-educated, vocationally successful individuals. Recent research findings indicate strongly that these goals are undeniably related to creativity.

It now seems possible that many things can be learned in creative ways more economically and effectively than by authority. It appears that children *can* be taught in such a way that their creative thinking abilities are useful in acquiring even the traditional educational skills, that these abilities are different from those measured by traditional intelligence and scholastic aptitude tests, and that they are important in mental health and vocational success.

Creativity may be defined in many ways. It is usually defined in terms of either a process or a product, but may also be defined in terms of a personality or an environmental condition. The author has chosen to define creativity as the process of sensing problems or gaps in information, forming ideas or hypotheses, testing and modifying these hypotheses, and communicating the results. This process may lead to any one of many kinds of products—verbal and nonverbal, concrete and abstract.

HOW IS CREATIVITY MANIFESTED AT DIFFERENT EDUCATIONAL LEVELS?

Early Childhood or Preschool Years

Many scholars have denied the possibility that young children can do productive thinking (producing something from what is cognized and remembered), and this has led to an overestimate of the child's receptivity. This misconception has led to an over-emphasis upon the importance of providing a *stimulating environment* to the neglect of providing a *responsive environment,* an emphasis upon recall and reproduction to the neglect of problem solving, creative thinking, and decision making. The beginnings of creative thinking may be found in the manipulative, exploratory, and experimental activities of the infant and the use of facial expressions, efforts to discover and test the meaning of facial expressions and gestures of others, and the like.

The Elementary School Years

Of the many manifestations of creativity during the elementary school years, greatest attention has been given to creative writing and art. We are now having a renewed recognition of the value of children's writing and art and discovering that children can be creative in a variety of other ways which are also important. Generally, educators of the past have considered children in the elementary and even in the high school years to be incapable of creative scientific thought; science has now been added to the elementary curriculum. In such fields as history, children are being taught the thinking skills of the historian. Similar developments have been forthcoming in anthropology, geography, psychology, and sociology.

The High School Years

A number of teen-agers have made history with their inventions, scientific discoveries, and other creative contributions. Among them are Arturo Toscanini, Wernher von Braun, Samuel Colt, Louis Braille, Galileo Galilei, and Edna St. Vincent Millay. Each year, a number of notable inventions and discoveries are credited to high school youths. High schools have long had provisions for recognizing creative writing and speaking talent and in recent years have been making provisions for recognizing scientific and inventive talent.

College Years

Undergraduate college students have been known to produce almost all types of creative products such as inventions, medical discoveries, books, monographs, dramas, and operas. Usually, however, such accomplishments have been achieved outside of college requirements and sponsorship. Dissertations and theses, usually regarded as original contributions, tend to be evaluated in terms of correctness of methodology rather than in terms of originality, power, and worth of the ideas developed and tested. Through honors programs and other provisions for individual investigations, efforts are being increased to change this picture.

During the past 80 years or more, a variety of procedures have been developed for measuring some of the creative thinking abilities. Most of these measures have been used only in research, and only now are tests of creative thinking abilities becoming available for use in schools. It should be made explicit at this point that the weight of evidence indicates that creative thinking is not a unitary ability, but that a number of abilities are involved. Thus, attempts to develop a single index of creative thinking or a CQ (Creative Quotient) should be avoided. According to the most extensive research in this field, the abilities involved are sensitivity to problems, fluency (the ability to produce a large number of ideas), flexibility (the ability to produce a variety of ideas or use a variety of approaches), originality (the ability to produce ideas that are off the beaten track), elaboration (the ability to fill in the details), and redefinition (the ability to define or perceive in a way different from the usual, established, or intended way, etc.).

Expanded Concept of the Human Mind

Perhaps one of the most important consequences thus far of the development and research use of measures of creative thinking has been an expanded concept of the human mind and its functioning. For many years, most people's concept of the human mind and its functioning was limited largely by the concepts embodied in intelligence tests. Developers of intelligence tests have not claimed that such tests assess all of a person's intellectual functioning. Yet, an intelligence or scholastic aptitude test has almost always been used by schools and clinics as the sole index of a person's intellectual potential. If her/his achievement in some area fell below the level which would be expected from her/his IQ, she/he was said to be underachieving. If a student achieved at an age level higher than would be expected from her/his IQ, she/he was somehow supposed to be overachieving. Curriculums and methods of teaching generally have been designed to bring about the kinds of growth or achievement related to the mental abilities involved in intelligence or scholastic aptitude tests. Tests of educational achievement likewise have been constructed along the same lines. This narrow concept of the human mind and its functioning has produced a kind of education which falls far short of our ideal of a humane education which will give all children a chance to realize their potentialities.

Non-test Ways of Identifying Creative Behavior

It will be some time before existing tests of creativity will be in common use. Many schools do not have school psychologists, counselors, or others qualified to use such tests. Also, a few children are not motivated to perform creatively on tests. Tests almost always have time limits, and creativity cannot always be hurried or forced. Some highly creative children have difficulty in writing their ideas, while others have special difficulty in communicating them orally. Thus, there is a need to continue to develop non-test ways of identifying creative talent.

Most teachers, however, have to redefine their customary concepts and values before they can identify creatively gifted pupils. When asked to evaluate pupils in terms of specific criteria of creativity, teachers generally report that this is the first time they have thought of their pupils in these terms. Much behavior that manifests the presence of creative talent is labeled by parents and classroom teachers as undesirable. One boy was so clever and ingenious in the way he cheated on a test that his teacher recognized his talent and was challenged to modify his teaching methods. The resulting change in the teacher's behavior was accompanied by dramatic changes in the boy's behavior and by the development of an outstanding talent.

One study revealed that the most frequently named non-test ways of idenifying creative talent by teachers are indicators of curiosity, inquisitiveness, investigativeness, and penetrating questioning. One rather well-validated set of indicators of curiosity includes "positive reactions to new, strange, incongruous, or mysterious elements in the environment (exploration, manipulation, etc.); exhibition of a need or desire to know about one's self and/or one's environment; scanning of one's surroundings seeking new experiences; and persistence in examining and exploring stimuli in order to know more about them."

Other frequently listed non-test indicators include originality in behavior (e.g., unusual solutions, unusual answers, and unusual approaches to problem solving); independent, individualistic, courageous behavior; imagination (e.g., fantasy and storytelling); nonconforming behavior (not bothered by pressures to conformity); unusual perceptiveness of relationships; an overflow of ideas; experimentation; unusual flexibility in meeting emergencies; unwillingness to give up; constructiveness; day-dreaming and preoccupation with an idea or problem; and going beyond assigned tasks.

WHAT IS MEANT BY CREATIVE WAYS OF LEARNING?

In this writer's opinion, the weight of present evidence indicates that people fundamentally prefer to learn in creative ways—by exploring, manipulating, questioning, experimenting, risking, testing, and modifying ideas. Teachers generally have insisted that it is more economical to learn by authority. Recent research suggests that many things, though not all, can be learned more effectively and economically in creative ways rather than by authority. It also appears that many individuals have an especially strong preference for learning creatively, learn a great deal if permitted to use their creative thinking abilities, and make little educational progress when we insist that they learn by authority. Such suggestions open existing possibilities for better ways of individualizing instruction.

Learning creatively takes place in the process of sensing problems or gaps in information, making guesses or hypotheses about these deficiencies, testing these guesses, revising and retesting them, and communicating the results. Strong human needs are involved in each stage of this process. If we sense that something is missing or untrue, tension is aroused. We are uncomfortable and want to do something to relieve the tension. This makes us want to ask questions, make guesses, or otherwise inquire. Uncertain as to whether our guesses are correct, we continue to be uncomfortable. Thus, we are driven to test our guesses, correct our errors, and modify our conclusions. Once we discover something, we want to tell someone about it. This is why it is so natural for human beings to learn creatively. It seems so spontaneous that some people call it incidental learning.

We learn by authority when we are told what we should learn and when we accept something as true because an authority says that it is. The authority may be a classroom teacher, or parent.

WHAT CAN TEACHERS DO?

At an early age many children appear to develop a preference for learning by authority. The human needs that make creative learning a natural process, however, appear to be sufficiently universal to make this way of learning a powerful one for all children, though not an exclusive one. What, then, can teachers do to provide the conditions in which the creative thinking abilities have a predominant role?

Provide Opportunities for Creative Behavior

One of the most obvious ways of providing conditions for creative learning is to offer a curriculum with plenty of opportunities for creative behavior. This can be done in many ways. It can be done by making assignments which call for original work, independent learning, self-initiated projects, and experimentation. It can be done daily by the kinds of questions teachers ask in class and by the kinds of problems used for discussion. The research evidence in favor of deliberate efforts to improve the quantity and quality of creative thinking are quite impressive.

Educational research has indicated repeatedly that people tend to learn along the lines they find rewarding. If we want children to think creatively, we must learn how to reward creative behavior. We reward children not only through grades but also through the kinds of behaviors we encourage or discourage and by the way we respond to the curiosity needs of children and young people.

We need to be respectful of the unusual questions children ask.

We must be respectful of the unusual ideas and solutions of children.

We need to show children that their ideas have value.

We need to provide opportunities and give credit for self-initiated learning.

We also need to provide chances for children to learn, think, and discover without threats of immediate evaluation.

Establish Creative Relationships with Children

All efforts to establish conditions for creative learning may fail unless classroom teachers are able to establish creative relationships with children.

The creative relationship between the teacher and pupil requires a willingness on the part of the teacher to permit one thing to lead to another, to embark with the child on an unknown adventure. It is also like the creative thinking process in that the teacher may work hard to establish this kind of relationship, may fervently want it, and still may fail. Then suddenly, it seems to "just happen." The teacher has to be ready to accept the relationship when it "happens," just as the inventor or scientific discoverer has to do. This aspect of the relationship, if nothing else, makes it vastly different from what is frequently referred to as permissiveness in education. The environment created by the teacher is definitely a responsive one in which the child finds adequate guidance.

Other Things Teachers Can Do

Although each teacher must evolve her/his own unique ways of teaching, experimental studies show that the following principles or procedures have positive value in facilitating creative behavior.

1. *Give purpose to creative writing. There is a difference in writing something to be corrected and writing something to be communicated.*

2. *Provide experiences which make children more sensitive to environmental stimuli.*

3. *Develop a constructive attitude toward the information taught.* Students who assume a constructive rather than a critical attitude toward available information were able to produce a larger number of creative solutions and more original ones.

4. *Provide adequate warm-up for creative activities.*

5. *In warming up pupils for creative thinking, avoid giving examples or illustrations which will freeze or unduly shape their thinking.*

6. *Avoid giving evaluative comments too frequently during practice problems or activities.*

7. *Provide unevaluated ("off-the-record") practice.* Young children are sometimes unproductive in responding to tests or creative thinking until they are urged to give their ideas "just for fun" or assured that "this doesn't count."

8. *Avoid the use of critical peer evaluation during practice sessions, especially above the third grade.*

9. *Within heterogeneous classes, use homogeneous rather than heterogeneous groupings occasionally to reduce the social stress among members of small groups working on creative group activities.*

10. *To evoke originality in thinking, make it clear that such thinking is expected and will be rewarded.*

WHAT ARE THE MOST COMMON BLOCKS TO CREATIVE DEVELOPMENT?

Although a great deal of research remains to be done concerning the inhibitors and facilitators of creative development, a few of them appear clear.

Inhibitors in Early Childhood

Perhaps the biggest task in nurturing creativity during the pre-school years is to keep alive fantasy until the child's intellectual development is such that she/he can engage in a sound type of creative thinking. The trouble is not that the child is eager to give up fantasy, but that there are pressures upon the child from all sides to be realistic and to stop imagining. At least since the early 1900's, investigators have been rather consistent in their recommendations concerning appropriate action, but the evidence indicates that the influence of these recommendations has been negligible.

Frequently investigators have also called attention to the stifling effects of "holding back operations," such as preventing children from learning more than they are "ready" to learn, attempting prematurely to eliminate fantasy, and overemphasizing sex roles.

Blocks During the Elementary School Years

Teachers face truly difficult problems in coping with the blocks to creative thinking during the elementary school years. Social expectations of what kind of behavior should or should not be permitted are powerful. One of the difficulties of the teachers is to reconcile spontaneity, initiative, and creativity in the classroom with the maintenance of discipline. Teachers frequently find creative children threatening to their status and security and disconcerting to classroom procedures. Some of the promising concepts now undergoing experimental testing may help teachers resolve their dilemmas. These include provisions for student's self-initiated learning, learning on one's own, a responsive environment rather than just a stimulating one, revisions of readiness concepts, the development of more realistic and favorable self-concepts, recognition of the uniqueness of the individual, and the development of the roles of specialists such as counselors, psychologists, and social workers.

The social forces most frequently mentioned by investigators as blocks to creative development include an extremely peer-oriented culture which emphasizes conformity to peer-group norms in behavior, sanctions against questioning and exploration, a success-oriented culture which makes errors fatal and makes children afraid to take a chance on trying a new approach, over-emphasis or misplaced emphasis on sex-role differences, the equation of divergency with abnormality or delinquency, and a sharp division between work and play.

Blocks During the High School and College Years

Most of the blocks present during the elementary period are also present during the high school years. Studies of adolescents have provided additional clues concerning other blocks within families which do not value or understand creative youngsters; in the adolescent culture which may place its greatest values on athletic prowess, being a "ladies' man," or achieving high grades; the values of teachers on conformity, security, "playing it safe," and completing work on time; emphases on conventional career choices; and popular but erroneous images of the creative scientists. Unusual strides have been made in the development of curricular materials especially in the sciences, mathematics, and social sciences which place much emphasis upon discovery, thinking, and imagination.

The most frequently mentioned blocks to creativity at the college level include *overemphasis* upon the acquisition of knowledge, memorization of facts, and finding already known answers to problems; the closely prescribed curriculum and bookkeeping system of credits; over-reliance upon textbooks and trust in authority; sacrifice of deep and genuine involvement to the coverage of subject matter; the lecture system of teaching; postponement for a readiness which never quite arrives, departmentalization and vested interests; expertness and specialization; the conviction that education should use only materials which are true, moral, or artistically excellent; mechanization and loss of intimacy between teachers and students; the conviction that education should be made as easy as possible; and the low prestige in our society of scholars, teachers, and research workers.

WHAT SHOULD BE THE GOALS IN GUIDING CREATIVITY?

Understanding, measuring, and developing the creative thinking abilities are part of the educator's great dream of achieving a more humane kind of education in which every child will have a better chance to achieve her/his potentialities. It is of obvious importance to society that creative talent be identified, developed, and utilized. Already, the understandings derived from research concerning the creative

55

thinking abilities have broadened our concepts of "gifted-ness" from that of the "child with the high IQ" to include also the highly creative child and perhaps other types. It is becoming increasingly clear that nothing can contribute more to mental health and the general welfare of our nation and to the satisfactions of its people than a general raising of the level of creativity. There is little doubt that the stifling of creative thinking cuts at the very roots of satisfaction in living and eventually creates overwhelming tension and break-down.

It has already been pointed out that the creative think-ing abilities are important in the acquisition of even the tradi-tionally measured kinds of achievement when children are permitted to achieve some of these goals in creative ways. Their importance in vocational success has also been men-tioned. Goals become clearer and more urgent, however, when we look upon the creative thinking abilities as just one part of our expanded and expanding concept of the human mind and its functioning. An acceptance of this broader con-cept of the human mind opens up many new and tremen-dously exciting possibilities for teachers. It places a new emphasis upon consideration of what human beings may be-come. It suggests that we can educate to a higher degree many people whom we have not been very successful in edu-cating. As we have begun to understand more deeply the creative functioning of the mind, the case for learning cre-atively rather than just by authority has been strengthened. This may soon enable us to learn what it really means to individualize instruction.

No matter how successful research becomes in deter-mining methods of identifying and developing creative talent in the child, teachers must never forget that the very life and function of creativity is to go courageously into the darkness of the unknown. This involves ever searching for the truth and living honestly. We shall be handicapped in achieving such a goal as long as we condition children to authority acceptance and dishonesty in the home, school, church, and government. The truly creative person, the kind of creative person that we need so urgently, must be able to make judgments independently and stick to them, even though most others disagree. It must be remembered that every new idea in the beginning always makes its originator a minority of one. It is well known from research that being a minority of one is tremendously uncomfortable and more than most people can tolerate. Thus, creativity takes great courage.

Unfortunately, the results of research are not encouraging when it comes to attitudes about the importance of courage. Teachers and parents in the United States do not give a place of great importance to either independence in judgment or courage, according to what they consider an ideal pupil. Obviously, such a pattern of values is more likely to produce a people ready for brainwashing than one able to resist it and to think creatively.

The characteristic rated at the top of the list by both parents and teachers in the United States is "consideration of others," certainly a valuable one. This preoccupation with consideration of others or politeness has been noted by a number of foreign observers who have lived in the United States. In their experiences, they found that this preoccupation causes us to be dishonest in our dealings with others and with each other. It causes us, in politeness, to promise things which we have no intention of doing. The characteristics of eminent creative persons as revealed through research would certainly suggest that anything which conditions children for dishonesty endangers creativity.

The Group: An Asset or a Liability to Learning?

by Louis M. Smith

Although social psychologists have theoretical disagreements as to the nature of a group, most would agree with the substance of the following definition: "A group is a social unit which consists of a number of individuals who interact with each other, who hold a common set of values, and who are interdependent."

Webster gives several definitions of *process,* of which the most applicable is: ". . . any phenomenon which shows a continuous change in time." Group processes, then, are the changes in this social unit—the group—that take place over a period of time. As these are described, concepts of group structure, roles, norms, and activities will be introduced to give further meaning to the definition. For our purposes the classroom teacher and her/his pupils will constitute the "classroom group," and the discussion will attempt to draw generalizations about the functioning of the classroom group.

THE INFORMAL STRUCTURE AND FUNCTIONING OF THE GROUP

Are there typical patterns in the organization and functioning of children's groups? Are there individual differences among groups of children? How can one discover the nature of the group?

The Sociometric Tests

Beginning 45 years ago two groups of investigators, working independently, developed and formalized the beginnings of what has come to be called *sociometry.* In one instance groups of children were asked to state their preferences for work and play companions. These nominations were then plotted into figures called sociograms, showing the interrelationships among children's choices. At about the same time a religious-education inquiry concerning the nature and development of children's character was being undertaken. The investigators asked children to "Guess Who?" among their classmates fit social and behavioral descriptions such as, "Who is the most honest boy?" and "Which girl works the hardest?" From both lines of inquiry have come a succession of important studies indicating structure of the classroom group, roles of the members, and norms possessed by groups.

Cliques and Subgroups

An immediate finding is that within a total classroom there are usually several informal, small clusters of students who like each other, who interact a good deal inside and outside of class, and who hold common beliefs about matters important to the children. The very real implication for the teacher is that any classroom group, in one sense, consists of many groups.

Several factors have been discovered; which account for the cleavage into small groups. First, boys usually choose their friends among boys, and girls usually choose girls. This situation is true at all levels, but particularly so in the middle elementary grades. This kind of self-segregation results from the sex roles stereo-typing practiced on children from infancy, both at home and at school. Second, the subgroups within the classroom will, as the students grow older, increasingly resemble the groupings within the community. Thus we find that the racial, religious, and socioeconomic differences of the community also occur in the classroom.

Several practical suggestions for the teacher's work have grown out of this knowledge and have been tested empirically. One writer has described "reassignment therapy" or, more simply, reseating the children in the classroom. For example, when a classroom contained a group of "disciplinary problems," the teacher had some ideas as to the individuals involved; the sociograms helped identify the closely attached clique *and also* indicated a few of the non-problem children liked by the problem children. The teacher regrouped the class so that each child could sit near a few friends but not near those involved in the difficulties. The class settled down and worked well after this. Reports, prepared by teachers trying to develop racial and religious tolerance, often point to the information about cleavages gained through use of sociometry as a measuring device, just as an achievement test gives evidence on accomplishment. Such information has been instrumental in planning future lessons, activities, and action.

Acceptance, Isolation, and Rejection

Another very typical research finding is the existence of individual differences among children who are liked or disliked. Differences in social acceptance seem less widely known than those in intelligence and reading achievements, for example. The writer has asked sixth-grade pupils to list the five or more children they like best and also the five or more children with whom they do not get along. A few children have had as many as 20 or 25 positive choices with no negative nominations, and others may have had just as many negative choices with no positive nominations. Typically, the range is much less.

Investigations of the correlates and reasons for one child being highly accepted or well liked, another being isolated, and a third being rejected, are numerous and reasonably consistent in results. "Acceptance" is positively correlated with intelligence, special abilities and skills, school achievement, socioeconomic status, and majority status in race and religion. The major relationships, however, are with personality characteristics indicative of good mental health and adjustment. Generally the well-liked children are adequately meeting life's problems and are responsible, independent, pleasant, and happy; such descriptions have been obtained from classroom teachers and also from the peers of pupils. The rejected children tend to have a variety of personal and social problems with which they are not coping successfully.

Within the limits of the stability of social ranking there is some evidence that teachers who work with isolated and rejected children do obtain some improvement. The techniques revolved around the assignment of classroom tasks which bring the individual into favorable interaction with classmates; assignment for group activities with any mutual choices or those whom the student chooses, and for the moment at least, not with those who reject her/him; and participation by the child in activities in which special skills can operate.

Special Roles .

The term "role" is applied to the behavior of a given individual in the scheme of interrelations within a group. In all groups, as individuals begin to interact and work toward common goals, certain responsibilities, behavior, and activity tend to be expected of particular individuals in the group. Just as this is true of siblings in large families and children in informal play and gang groups, it is true of classroom groups, and incidentally, of the subgroups within the classroom group. A teacher who is to understand individual behavior must look at the kinds of roles in the group, the satisfaction the roles bring to the individuals, the conflicts as to who is to play each role, and the specific behavioral prescriptions entailed by the roles.

Group Functioning

Although much investigation remains to be done in the area of internal group functioning, a few results of investigations of "contagion" will indicate the possibilities of research findings, as well as the possibilities of the critical application of group concepts by the teacher in thinking about her/his own classroom. Behavioral contagion is the spontaneous imitation by peers of a behavior initiated by a single group member, though that person may not have intended the peer group to imitate the behavior. By interrelating judgments regarding "who is able to influence the other fellow," and by direct observation of group behavior, investigators have found: contagion spreads more frequently *from* high-influence children; children who perceive another individual as powerful are most likely to be influenced by the other individual (as well as to accept direct attempts at influence); low-power members initiate nondirective influence attempts, and initiate deferential, approval-seeking behavior toward high figures. A teacher with such knowledge can understand and predict some of the group processes in her/his particular classroom.

Just as contagion is an immediate phenomenon appearing in all classrooms, so is the phenomenon of *conformity and deviation*. As described earlier, most children belong to subgroups in the class. As these subgroups formulate points of view about how the members in general and the child in particular should behave, then the child *must* acquiesce and conform. The verb "must" is used deliberately because of the consequences if the child does not conform. Research indicates that as a person deviates from the group standard, the group members initiate many direct attempts to influence her/him; the members soon terminate interaction and comment that the deviate is not wanted or wanted less (rejection); and finally, the more closely knit the group and the more critical the issue the more pronounced the influence attempts and rejection become. In effect, the group controls a good many rewards and punishments in the life of the child.

A final comment on the dynamics of the small group suggests an area requiring further analysis and application of research findings to classrooms. Teachers and group workers have commented frequently, ". . . it depends on the person or the personality of the individual pupil." If personality can be considered in a simplified manner as the constellation of motives and other dispositions to behave, several observations are in order. When individuals vary in their need for achievement, doing well, competing, succeeding, and need for affiliation, it would be expected that these individuals would show differences in their reaction to groups, and groups would react differently to them. Such as the case. The major recommendation to the classroom teacher follows logically: she/he must have a carefully acquired concept of human personality and be alert to its expression in individual pupils if she/he is to understand the relation of the individual to the group.

THE TEACHER AND THE GROUP

Because of the nature of the situation, the teacher is the leader of the group. Leadership is viewed here not in terms of personality, but in terms of two major roles, *initiating structure* and *consideration.*

Initiating structure refers to the following kinds of behaviors: makes the way she/he feels clear to the group, tries out new ideas, criticizes poor work, and emphasizes deadlines. In short, the leader, and the classroom teacher as a leader, is directive, takes action, coordinates work, makes decisions, and "initiates structure."

Good leaders also fill the second role consideration. This aspect has been called the "human relations" dimension of leader behavior and is typified by high ratings on such items as doing little things to make it pleasant to be a member of the group, finding time to listen to group members, explaining her/his actions, treating members as equals, being willing to make changes, getting group approval before going ahead, and looking out for the personal welfare of individual members.

Leaders who are high in the dimensions of *initiating structure* and *consideration* have "good" groups; that is, groups which reach their goals and groups which contribute satisfactions to the members. This generalization is one of the most important findings of psychological research in the group process area.

Implications for Teachers

The implications for "discipline" in the school classroom seem to fall into perspective from the leadership framework. Although some research emphasizes one dimension rather than another, both aspects of teacher behavior are important. At the high-school level one investigator grouped teachers into those who had serious problems in "classroom control" and those who had groups which moved along easily and well. He found the classes of the latter were characterized by vital and enthusiastic presentation of material, use of all available equipment and aids to enrich a lesson, and routine organization of procedures for mundane tasks such as distributing paper. Another study of discipline at the elementary level examined the teacher's behavior in handling specific but serious "disciplinary" problems during the course of the day. The teachers who had received high prior ratings as having cooperative, interested, and hard-working classes tended to interact with the children in a manner reflecting nonpunitiveness, concern with the discovery of the difficulty, and cooperative analysis and solution of the problem.

There have been several research illustrations of leaders who are high on consideration and low on initiating structure. From one study we summarized the outline of a graphic description; a picture of the learning situation and pupil-teacher relationship was obtained from evaluation sheets filled out by the pupils. The total impression was one of an impartial and cooperative teacher who helped the learners to get some new ideas, but who, despite the pleasant inter-personal relationships, did not help them sufficiently in identifying new problem areas and did not help them visualize the action possibilities arising from such problems. This teacher did not adequately *structure* the situation for the learners so that they could identify and work upon problems that were challenging to them and pertinent to their interests. Members of the class, in their evaluation scales, often wrote that they wasted their time and were bored, thereby indicating that the lack of structuring by the teacher frustrated many of them. The teacher seems to have related as an individual to the majority of the pupils, but this satisfactory social relationship failed to meet the needs and expectancies of the learners insofar as problem solving and learning activities were concerned.

When leaders are low in both dimensions, confusion and misbehavior seem to be the major results. Some investigators have found structure arising within the group when the nominal leader is out of the room.

Leader Behavior and the Classroom Group

There has been little research in desirable variations of leader behavior with different groups. The common teacher observation such as, ". . . my fifth-hour group is like no other group I've had . . ." implies that the group differs from others and the teacher should behave in a different manner. Precisely how this group differs and the corresponding necessary changes in the teacher's actions are important but virtually unanalyzed questions. In one very interesting study the investigators measured teachers on consideration, and had pupils rate the adequacy of the teachers. In those classes where the pupils were more task-oriented and had high needs for achievement, there was no relationship between the good teacher and amount of consideration. In those classes where the pupils were more person-oriented and had high needs for affiliation, the teachers with high consideration scores were rated as better.

Similar questions can be raised concerning groups which vary in age and maturity and in intellectual ability and socio-economic status. As the classroom composition of cliques, conflicting roles, and personalities vary, the most appropriate alternatives might also vary.

Research has given support to the idea that the group, structured by teacher expectations for problem solving and major participation, can help the individual pupil develop skills in critical and independent thought. This point of view has been an underlying assumption in much educational writing supporting "group work." A further basic assumption, not so carefully analyzed, is that this freedom of thought and judgment in the developing child is freedom from excessive dependence on adults and freedom from the traditional authority of the textbook. Apparently—and here the writer has no evidence—individuals who have looked to the benefits of this kind of freedom have seen it as the most critical and difficult problem in the intellectual development of children. These individuals believe that the classroom group can give the child strength and training in moving toward more mature judgment.

Other writers think that the peer group may be a serious obstacle facing the individual in the development and main-teanance of independent thought and action. That the group can have a negative effect on simple individual judgments has been shown, e.g., an investigator instructed eight individuals to judge simple perceptual relations; that is, to match a given line with one of three unequal lines. In the course of making an oral report of his judgment, one individual found himself contradicted by each of the preceding seven members. This contradiction was repeated again and again in the experi-ment. The other seven members who had been instructed to behave in the "wrong way" were all consistent in their state-ments and unanimously and clearly contradicted the judg-ment of the one individual. The results indicate that one-third of the estimates made by the last member became errors in the direction of the majority. Those who remained independent did so with considerable conflict and stress. Those who yielded were of several types: some yielded with-out realizing they were yielding; some yielded with self-doubt about their own perception; and some yielded, not because they doubted themselves, but because they were reluctant to deviate overtly. If this compromising of judgment occurs one-third of the time in simple perceptual judgments, what are the consequences when dealing with more abstract and ambiguous intellectual problems? Can the peer group come to exercise a tyranny over the individual as well as free her/him from more traditional authority?

Other Individual Learning

The effects of group experience upon the content of one's values and ideology is pervasive and thorough. Beyond the ever-present data from culture to culture and social class to social class, there have been many research and case study reports of a group's influence on attitudes and personal-social behavior. This learning or socialization process involves an initial awareness and knowledge of the group norms and social values. As the child interacts with group members, this awareness of outside values shifts to an internalization and an acceptance of the values. Social psychologists describe the process as following certain steps: (1) in group relations the child comes to see that rules or norms are based on mutual agreements; (2) she/he finds that rules can be changed or new rules can be made; and (3) as she/he begins to take part in the process of changing and making the rules, they become the child's *own* rules. The key factor in acceptance of rules or norms is *participation* in the process and actions of the group.

By such a process as the one described the child comes to develop a set of attitudes and values characteristic of the group. In the classroom the possible influences of the subgroup norms and teacher attitudes are apparent, as are the possible conflicts among various influences.

BASIC IDEAS FOR USE

The generalizations suggested to the classroom teacher by research in group processes can be briefly summarized as follows:

1. The classroom can be considered a group, albeit a special kind of group, with goals involving the accomplishment of certain tasks as well as intragroup harmony and personal satisfaction. The group tasks eventually resolve into individual pupil learning.

2. Although the classroom group is a single group, it also contains a number of subgroups which may or may not be in harmony. Within each classroom there is variability in acceptance and rejection of individual members. There are various roles, special patterns of behavior filled by specific individuals.

3. The interaction of the classroom teacher with the group is most aptly described by the concept of leadership. The good leader fills two major roles: *initiating structure* and *consideration*. In terms of these roles the teacher gives direction, sets standards, organizes activities, and is involved in all phases of group activities; and the teacher respects pupil ideas, suggestions, opinions, and personalities. An inability or refusal to meet these roles results in a classroom beset with interpersonal difficulty and lack of accomplishment of group tasks and work.

4. Specific individual learning is dependent, of course, on the content of the activities instituted by the classroom teacher, but also on the nature of the group and the teacher's leadership behavior. The group and the leader exert influences directly on pupil motivation, action, and learning. That group influences directly affect behavior is especially clear in critical thinking, attitude development, and social skills.

Group Interaction: A Significant Force in Learning

by Jean D. Grambs

People differ, and they differ in important ways. More-over, these differences have contributed significantly to the rich diversity of American life. Only when there is respect for differences can freedom flourish vigorously—a well-recognized principle of American democracy. Nevertheless, an individual may often find herself/himself at once attracted and repulsed by differences, particularly by the differences of a group unlike her/his own. This ambivalence, which is often conveyed to children and growing youth, may prove to be the source of conflict and tension between groups.

THE NATURE OF GROUPS

People Belong to One Biological Family

One of the facts about which we can have some certainty is that people, wherever they may be found, belong to one biological family, *homo sapiens*. However, individuals do differ, as we can see when we look around us. There are fairly distinct "races" that differ from each other in recognizable fashion. How did these differences occur? Physical anthropologists, biologists, and others who have studied the evolution of human beings tell us that the variations in human appearance have occurred as adaptations to different surroundings. Isolation of groups of people led to selective repetition of those genes and chromosomes that determine skin color, hair quality and color, eye color, and eye shape. Yet, such differences are not significant in terms of a common inheritance of human physiology. There appears to be little doubt that human geings actually evolved as a distinctive species only once; the physical differences we observe in each other are variations on the same basic human theme.

Upon the common inheritance of a thinking brain, a consciousness of self, an ability to reason and to remember, human beings have built vast and complicated civilizations. These have differed tremendously, and yet in many instances have been—though separated by oceans—so similar as to startle the present-day observer. Fire, the calendar, the wheel, a written language, an ethical system, a concept of deity or deities, all of these can be found in various parts of the world, widely separated, yet remarkably similar. One can only speculate that the brain and unique quality of consciousness of self of the human being are the transcendent common characteristics, demonstrating once again that all people are, basically, part of the same genealogical family.

Ethnocentrism Is a Part of Group Development

The average "person on the street" (whatever the street may be) does not generally acknowledge a share of the same basic inheritance with members of other cultural groups, particularly if they are of another race. In numerous studies of primitive and of literate cultures, anthropologists have reported conclusive evidence that each group develops its own sense of self-esteem. We humans like what we do, we like what we are, we prefer the appearance of "our own people." These preferences are the building blocks of cultural diversity. Members of a group believe in the "rightness" of their own way of life, which is natural, for this way of life is what they know best. Moreover, when these individuals who are convinced of the absolute "rightness" of their own group are brought into contact with other groups, they are likely to regard the others with suspicion, perhaps mixed with fear. They observe other groups only from the vantage point of their own cultural base and conclude that different ways of doing things are probably inferior to their own way. This certainty of one's own group as the center of all culture and as the best way to organize one's life is called "ethnocentrism."

Insofar as ethnocentrism prevails, the individual will see herself/himself as "inside" the "right" culture, or group, and the other groups as "outside." In other words, she/he belongs to the "ingroup" and others belong to the "outgroup." Ingroups and outgroups may be found in the many subcultures that make up any given society. Research shows, for example, that clique and gang formation among adolescents almost always includes a "we-they" feeling: those who belong to our club, clique, or gang are good; those who do not belong or belong to another clique or gang are not good.

Ignorance is a potent factor in establishing one's own group as superior. In one study, when seven-year-old children were asked which were better, children in their town or those in a neighboring town, they invariably answered that the children in their own town were better. When asked why, the replied, "We don't know the other children."

We human beings prefer what we know, and until we are better informed, we all tend to act like these children and assume that what is unknown is not as good as what is known.

The Group Is the Ground We Stand On

Kurt Lewin, the astute social psychologist, made the statement that "the group is the ground we stand on." In other words, the social nature of human beings necessitates their belonging to a group in which they are accepted and have a functional role and whose ways of doing things are familiar and comfortable. Persons who lack a sense of group identity, according to Lewin and subsequent researchers in this field, are indeed insecure and shaky people.

Recent studies of delinquent behavior suggest that, to some extent, aggression and hostility derive from a lack of group identity, and a rootlessness that produces intense feelings of insecurity in the growing person. Unaware of the source of these feelings, the youngster may strike out aimlessly and wantonly at a world that has seemingly provided no safe and accepted ground for her/him to stand on. Whether in the city or in the suburbs, children do not know *what* they are, and, therefore, find it hard to know *who* they are; being immature, they know of few ways to react to such a psychological burden other than through anger and defense.

It is important to note here that group identification is not limited to an individual's racial or ethnic groups, for social-class differences also serve to differentiate individuals. One study of fifth- and sixth-grade pupils showed clearly that socioeconomic differences among typical white children led to attributing "better" characteristics to children from the upper economic class and "worse" characteristics to those from the lower economic groups. Ethnocentrism in terms of social class later leads to the sorting of adolescents into gangs and cliques, and it undoubtedly contributes to the much higher rate of dropouts and nonachievers among underprivileged youngsters who are demoralized by their "outcast" status.

For many young people, the group "upon which they stand" is a group that is socially downgraded. Many delinquents coming from minority groups have learned that their being Chicano or Puerto Rican or Polish or Black immediately lessens their value in the eyes of the prevailing society; they have found that many doors are automatically closed to them. Recognizing this, the youngster downgrades herself/himself and says, in effect: "If others think people like me are not very good, then probably I am not very good. Then why should I try? Why should I do what the teacher ask, when they aren't like me or my people at all?"

Groups Under Restrictive Social Controls

Particular groups, who are objects of discrimination and disparagement, often experience intergroup problems that extend far beyond the typical problems of "growing up" or "getting along with people." They are called "minority" groups, though in some instances they might be actual majorities. Yet in terms of access to power, to positions of status, to prestige, and to community leadership, most members of such minority groups are severely restricted.

The history of most minority groups in the United States is strikingly similar. All have started at the bottom of the socioeconomic ladder. Although some Chinese and Japanese have now become well-to-do business and professional people, there was a long period when immigrants from Asia were at the bottom of the labor market. Today the immigrant Puerto Rican is the depressed minority group in New York City, while the Chicano is the minority group in the Southwest. As a group the Black has long been at the lowest socioeconomic level, although individual Blacks have, of course, achieved professional status and wealth. Most of the ethnic groups who arrived in the United States between 1850 and 1920 also have histories of starting in the tenement districts of big cities and being the despised and underpaid workers in the dirty and menial jobs of factory and mine. As one group manages, often through education, to move out of the worst slums and most depressed jobs, another group moves in. Housing officials have noted the "waves of succession" in the slum areas of cities.

Despite shifts in economic status, many minority groups are still the objects of discriminatory treatment. Jews, no matter what their income, will find themselves excluded from certain housing tracts, may not be able to get some jobs on an equal status with others, and are likely to find overt or hidden quota systems applied in college admissions. The same may be true of Catholics. Thus, the stigma of minority-group identification is not necessarily removed with an individual's rise in socioeconomic status.

INTERGROUP CONCEPTS OF PARTICULAR SIGNIFICANCE TO THE SCHOOL

With the current emphasis upon identifying the potential capacities of students, there has been an increased interest in the question: "Who is intelligent?" as well as "What is intelligence?" Classroom teachers have a primary responsibility for the guidance of young people. The classroom teacher encourages some students to enter intellectually difficult pursuits and directs others toward activities which require manual dexterity, artistic or creative ability, or other kinds of talent. The classroom teacher needs to know the educational potential of each student.

Intelligence tests are widely used as one means of determining the characteristics required in certain occupations. Many research workers have been interested in the question of innate intelligence versus intelligence conditioned by environmental factors. Today the question is still being subjected to the rigors of research analysis. On one point there is agreement among those best qualified to judge: there are no *innate* differences in intellectual potential among racial, ethnic, or religious groups.

Of course, there are many differences among individuals. One of the major differences is the *use* an individual may make of her/his potential. Probably the single most significant factor is socioeconomic status. A bright child growing up in a home where reading is despised, where few books, magazines, or newspapers are to be found, and where schooling is scorned will find it difficult to act like an "intelligent" child in school, where reading, intellectual achievement, and education are prized.

Careful studies of group intelligence tests have shown that these tests may have a "culture bias" that operates against youngsters from a poor or culturally impoverished environment. Such a child just does not *know* that a harp is like a piano because both have strings; she/he may never have seen either. Yet this and similar questions may be used in tests assessing her/his "intelligence." As has been pointed out, today's city children might appear to be "dumb" if compared with Eskimo children for their knowledge of the animals, seasons, and phenomena peculiar to the Artic region. A New York City report observed that it is not reasonable to measure the intelligence of Spanish-Speaking children with an English-language test whose content derives from mainland culture. For this reason, the New York City schools have used nonverbal intelligence tests, with instructions in Spanish, and achievement tests in Spanish to assess the intellectual potential and the functional educational level of Puerto Rican students.

Another factor of importance established by research is motivation. Children who find no appreciation at home for their achievement in tests are not likely to try very hard in test situations. Experiments with various kinds of motivations have shown that test scores can be improved or lowered according to the degree of reward or punishment the individual is led to expect. Thus, caution is necessary in accepting or assessing the results of tests that tend to characterize a whole group of students as either particularly low or particularly high in intelligence, since environmental factors may play a hidden but crucial role. Similarly, in guiding an individual's life choice, the teacher must use intelligence test scores with great care and only with expert advice.

A major focus of attention in recent years has been the assessing of differences in intellectual ability of Black and white students. According to a number of opinion polls, the average man on the street believes that Blacks are *innately* less intelligent than most whites. Research studies indicate that although in many situations the *average* scores of groups of Black children will be lower than those of similar groups of white children, there will be extensive overlapping of the individual scores. That is, some of the Black youngsters will obtain scores as high as those of high-ranking white youngsters, and some white youngsters will have scores as low as low-ranking youngsters in the Black group.

Careful analysis of the many research studies of intelligence differences among various racial groups has led a number of observers to the conclusion that these apparent differences in intellectual ability are to be accounted for primarily by two factors: environment and motivation.

Much data lends support to the hypothesis that there are no *innate* group differences in intelligence but that factors such as socioeconomic status, motivation, and environmental learning may account for group differences. A study of the origin of Black people of distinction has shown that a satistically significant number came from certain selected counties in the South. In these counties there were educational opportunities not available elsewhere for Blacks at that time. This evidence suggests that in identifying and educating talented students from minority groups, the school has a most important role, a role requiring careful scrutiny, for these youngsters may otherwise be overlooked or be without adequate guidance.

Children Recognize Group Differences

Many adults assume that children are not aware of racial, ethnic, or religious differences in other people. However, research does not bear out this supposition. Children mirror the world around them. The climate of opinion that affects children appears to be more pervasive than even personal contact. Studies of the attitudes of children and young people clearly show that children *do* recognize differences and that these "anti" feelings are related to the attitudes and feelings of adults.

The perception of group differences by very young children does not imply that a child is born with an innate awareness of these differences. These are *learned* perceptions. The newborn child does not know her/his group identity. Members of the child's family—often without conscious effort—impart to her/him their conceptions of their own worth as members of a particular racial, ethnic, or religious group and also indicate the other groups she/he may meet that are to be considered "good" and acceptable, or "bad" and not acceptable or to be feared. True or false, these notions about one's own group and about other groups are passed on from generation to generation.

Contemporary American culture reinforces many ideas about groups. The role of newspapers, television, and other mass media is probably crucial. Yet this kind of influence is extremely difficult to assess. The mass media have in the past presented a rather stereotyped image of certain groups in our society, e.g., the Italian peddler, the Black servant, and the Irish cop. A study of magazine fiction showed, for instance, that most of the characters were Anglo-Saxon American, while members of non-Anglo-Saxon minority groups, when they appeared, were usually in minor roles, came from low socioeconomic positions, and did not possess wholly desirable characteristics. A study of over 100 motion pictures showed that in over three-fourths of the cases the Black was presented in terms of the stereotype of the Black or in a disparaging manner; only 12 percent of the Black characters were presented in a favorable light.

Studies of textbooks have shown that descriptions of different groups within the United States are surrounded by "good" ideas and symbols, while others are surrounded by "bad" concepts. For instance, the early immigrants in the years before 1880 have often been described in textbooks as pioneers and homesteaders who broke new ground with courage and determination. Those who came after 1880 were often associated with such terms as "swarms of immigrants" or "teeming hordes." Pupils reading such descriptions may accept these designations uncritically and unconsciously.

Studies of textbooks have also revealed that the Black, as a slave, has been given a large amount of space, and the conditions of slavery have been described in detail often with stress on the benign aspects of slavery. After the discussion of the Reconstruction Period, the Black as a group in American life drops out of sight. What impression of Black life and character will students then retain? Newer instructional materials attempt to give more accurate portrayals of groups and individuals in both text and supplementary books. Such stereotypes as the "sly Chinese," the "lazy Mexican," the "cute little pickaninny" are fast disappearing from children's literature and school texts.

Some Children Become More Prejudiced Than Others

A large body of research literature has been devoted to prejudices and their formation. Prejudice, as the word itself indicates, means "prejudging." A prejudice may be against a person, a place, a kind of food ("I won't eat oysters; no, of course, I've never tried them!"), wearing apparel, words, or almost anything. The necessary element in any prejudice is that the person holding it is not at all inclined to test her/his prejudice against experience or to be influenced by facts that are contrary to her/his own beliefs.

One of the most interesting findings in recent research is that some people appear to be more prejudiced than others in the same general environment. Where prejudice does exist—particularly when it occurs in children and is directed toward other children—it seems to be related to such personality characteristics as cynicism, fearfulness, hostility, suspiciousness, and a lack of confidence and security.

Children from homes lacking in warmth and affection, where punishment is rigid and harsh, are more apt to have strong feelings of dislike for people unlike themselves. A lack of self-acceptance in a child has been found to be closely associated with inability to adjust adequately to children of either one's own group or another. One's concept of self is a significant factor in accepting or rejecting others. There seems to be firm ground upon which to base the statement that children who do not like themselves are ones who will, unless helped, find it difficult to learn to like others.

The Feeling of Difference Is Important

The feeling of difference, as it affects children and adolescents, is of crucial concern to educators. Behavior in classroom and school that might seem bizarre or unacceptable to the typical teacher may actually come out of the underworld of youthful tensions and intergroup conflicts, where words hurt and damage. To be "in" with the right group (or wrong group, as the case may be) is of urgent significance during these years of growing up. And if someone calls a teen-ager a "dirty Mex," the person called such a name may retaliate by misbehavior, by wearing extreme clothing, or even by physical violence.

Being a member of a minority group in our present-day society is not easy. What does it mean, for instance, to a Black child to grow up in a predominantly white world? Case studies suggest that no Black children escape the "moment of revelation" when they recognize the fact of their inescapable difference, a difference that they cannot erase by changing a name or attending a different church or marrying a rich wife. The difference is physical and obvious. Although the same feeling of difference is often experienced by Chinese and Japanese children, they have learned from their parents that theirs is a respected and honored culture worthy of group identification. But the Blacks, among the oldest of America's population groups, have only recently begun to look back to African forebears. The very process of forced migration and tribal and family dislocation left them with only American cultural forms to learn and adopt. It is interesting to note that in one research study a group of deprived and educationally resistant Black children responded actively to the school's program during the study of Negro History Week; this experience gave them a feeling of self-respect which, in turn, brought both better class behavior and an increase in their learning.

The current interst in developing materials and units on Black history at all grade levels is too new to have been assessed adequately. However, teachers have found Black students responding with great interest to data on their own past, and also to new archaeological and historical material regarding ancient African cultures. Similarly, white students, especially in Northern or Southern segregated areas, have been startled to new awareness by exposure to the same material on the Black.

The children of foreign-born parents, particularly if English is not the primary language at home, are affected by other group pressures and differences. From their parents they learn manners, food habits, family role relationships, attitudes toward education and the future, and these may differ in many respects from those of the American school and of the American culture as conveyed through the mass media. To what shall these children be loyal? If they reject their parents' attitudes and values, they feel highly insecure and uncertain and are inevitably involved in conflict and trouble at home. If they do not accept the school's version of what is "American," they are apt to be left out of school activities, to receive poor grades, and in many crude or subtle ways to be made to feel unworthy. They may avoid conflict in school by adopting the school's image of an American child and be rewarded by the school, but then they may be punished by their parents. This is, indeed, a cruel dilemma.

Many millions of Americans have had the "second-generation" experience, and their stories have been told in books of biography, autobiography, and fiction. Today, with a decline in immigration, the second-generation problem affects fewer young people. In a few large Northern and Midwestern cities and certain agricultural areas, groups of Puerto Ricans, Chicanos, Appalachian whites, and rural Southern Blacks are now caught in second-generation situations, both bilingual and bicultural, that will remain acute for many years.

Differences Should Be Prized

To feel different and to feel superior is one thing; to feel different and to feel inferior is quite another. Probably, the central problem of intergroup education revolves around this factor more than any other. If differences were not demeaning, each person would prize differences.

As the study of society becomes more truly scientific, increasingly it appears that certain social values which at one time had a justifiable rationale survive today as little more than residual social habits. It is also clear that many individuals gain self-enhancement by looking down on or deriding others. Most people will acknowledge that the shape of a person's eyes or a persion's religion will not tell them whether she/he is loyal, trustworthy, honest, or talented; yet for irrelevant reasons such as appearance a person may be deprived of educational and social opportunities. The explanation of this behavior, psychologists say, may lie in the individual's need to feel secure and worthy. When an individual does not have status in the world of reality, she/he seeks it through artificial or imaginary means. The practice of finding a "scapegoat" is one form of discriminatory behavior; by this means, individuals pay back the world for the kicks given to them. They kick those who are weaker than themselves and thus transmit to others their own unpleasant feeling toward the world. This psychological mechanism seems to operate when one child picks on a less agile child or derides a child from a minority group. Usually, the victim has done nothing except to exist.

INTERGROUP EDUCATION: SOME GUIDELINES TO PRACTICE

It is generally acknowledged today that school programs cannot ignore the group differences that children bring to school. If the school ignores them, the children do not. School yard and gang fights, painful ostracism from school activities, the florishing of secret societies, often stem from lack of school programs designed to build acceptance of group differences.

Each school faculty will find it important to know the community from which the children come. What are the racial, ethnic, and socioeconomic groups in its community? is there tension among these groups? What are the social rankings assigned to each group by the community? Answers to these questions will help the faculty recognize what kinds of intergroup understandings may be most needed in its school.

The components of attitudes have not yet been perfectly defined, nor can one always be sure of the particular key to attitude change. Our present knowledge suggests certain desirable school practices:

1. *Healthy group relationships are promoted when invidious comparisons are eliminated.*

2. *Changes in attitude are also changes in feelings. A judicious combination of both fact and ethical considerations does help individuals reassess their own beliefs and attitudes, and thus change.*

3. *Individuals, whether children or adults, may be helped to change their attitudes about others through specific kinds of direct experience.* (If pupils think that all Chinese work in laundries, this stereotype can be modified by bring to class a Chinese-A .ierican doctor, dentist, lawyer, engineer, or teacher. However, such persons are brought to the classroom not because they are Chinese-Americans, but because they can tell something important about their job or profession. The skillful teacher later utilizes the situation to point out that the stereotype of "all Chinese work in laundries" just doesn't hold up.)

4. *Experiencing an intergroup situation does not necessarily affect the attitudes of those involved. Teachers must make the facts explicit by helping children to see "we are learning about how people differ" and by showing that such differences require serious thought.*

5. *Children should see and learn about minority-group individuals who have achieved high social status and prestige.*

6. *Surface behavior and under-the-surface feelings may be quite different.*

7. *Children and youth need help in acquiring understanding of how it feels to be in the other person's shoes.*

8. *Teachers can use to advantage even the fights and clashes that disturb and disrupt school situations. The fact that there is intergroup hostility in a school may properly become important teaching content within the classroom. Using methods of problem solving which involve data gathering, testing of myths against reality, and establishing hypotheses and alternative solutions will aid children and youth to develop reasonable behaviors in regard to other individuals and groups.*

Disadvantaged Groups: A Special Challenge

by Gertrude Noar

The children most often referred to as *disadvantaged* are the result of poverty: the city slum-dwellers, rural uneducated farmhands, and migrants. They are the children of unassimilated lower social class Blacks, Caucasians, Puerto Ricans, First Americans, and Chicanos. They are a growing percentage of children who have too little of everything: too little living space, too little food and sleep, too little personal attention, too little medical and nursing care, too little energy and endurance, too little information about themselves and their world, too little curiosity (why ask when no one answers?), too little success.

Current writers and researchers tend to use a much more inclusive definition. According to Mario D. Fantini and Gerald Weinstein, "the meaning of the term 'disadvantaged' must be broadened to include all those who are blocked in any way from fulfilling their human potential." This definition includes children whose cultural background is so different from middle-class American culture that they are unable to succeed in the classroom. In current usage, the term *disadvantaged* refers to any child whose needs the school fails to meet.

SUBCULTURE GROUPS

Students whose cultural backgrounds are different from middle-class school culture may be thought of as disadvantaged in the sense that their value and culture patterns, and perhaps their language, make their behavior different from that expected by many teachers. For example, First American children are not likely to talk to or smile at people they do not know. They are easily embarrassed by being singled out for praise.

A minority group whose educational problems are presently receiving increased attention is the Chicano migrant workers. The children of families of similar extraction who have settled permanently in cities like Denver and Albuquerque also present problems to teachers who do not understand their traditional family relationships (male domination, for example) and negative attitudes toward education beyond compulsory school age (especially for girls). Many families speak only Spanish, which presents a problem of communication for those teachers who speak only English.

Some educators believe that these children should be taught Spanish first, for many speak and write it poorly. Others suggest that they should be taught all subjects in Spanish, especially in the primary grades. Although teachers generally accept the idea that English should be taught as a second language, many seem not to know what that requires. There is evidence that when their teachers do understand and speak at least some Spanish, the children feel better about their language, their families, their heritage, and themselves. When Spanish is forbidden in school, these children develop feelings of shame and guilt. Consequent anxiety and a sense of inadequacy block learning.

For similar reasons, Puerto Rican children benefit when their teachers are able to understand and speak some Spanish. These teachers also need to know about living conditions, values, behavior patterns, and traditions in Puerto Rico, for many families are first generation here.

The education establishment in this country is now deeply concerned with development of minority group children no matter where they live or what makes them different. Attention is being given to what they learn in the schools they now attend and to what relevance that learning has to their present lives. Up to now, except where courageous teachers have tried innovations, there has been too little connection between school and the events in their world, and the little most of these children learn in school is soon forgotten.

WHAT DISADVANTAGED CHILDREN ARE LIKE IN SCHOOL AND WHAT THEIR BEHAVIOR MEANS

Many disadvantaged children tend to behave differently from what the teacher demands. In class they talk out, fool around, play tricks, tap feet and pencils, make noise, don't sit still, and screen out the teacher's voice. Teachers often call them babyish. However, much of this behavior is more likely to stem from frustration, which, coupled with anxiety, may make a child cry or eat in class. Frustration may also cause a child to jerk paper out of a notebook and crumple up piece after piece as she/he makes new attempts to do her/his work.

Torn, rumpled, unorganized notebooks and desks filled with bits of food, candy wrappers, and pencil stubs are common among these pupils. Many teachers are repelled by this and tend to describe the children as dirty and disorganized. However, unlike middle-class children, the children of poverty are less able to learn to organize anything if their living quarters are crowded with people, if there is no furniture with drawers, if there are no kitchens with cupboards and no bedrooms with closets.

Some teachers believe that Black children steal more than others. Stealing is not a racial characteristic. It is a complex behavior stemming from a variety of causes which cannot be fully described here. All children have to be taught not to take what belongs to others. Most lower-class young children never own anything. In their families each one takes what she/he needs from the common and usually inadequate supply of food and clothing in the home.

Many disadvantaged children, especially in secondary schools, seem to be suspicious, to carry a chip on the shoulder, to feel picked on. They may pull away from and resent a teacher who in all friendliness puts a hand on them. Teachers get upset and angry about this. It may enforce the fear of Blacks which some teachers feel and increase their resentment at having to teach in center-city schools. It is important, when dealing with such a child, to remember that many Black children are brought up to fear white people, to regard the white teacher (an authority figure) as an enemy. They have heard about and have seen on TV the cruel mistreatment of teenagers, even younger children, and adults by police and white bystanders in civil rights demonstrations. They hear talk about beatings and killings that were never reported in the news. They know that some Black children have been beaten up when they attempted to go to white schools. It takes patience, kindness, understanding, and many good experiencs for teachers to convince such children of their fairness and friendship. Some middle-class Black teachers also resent teaching lower-class children who may reject them. Similarity of race does not guarantee acceptance or understanding.

Many disadvantaged children are not oriented to tests, promptness, time, speed, or competition. This does not usually indicate laziness, indifference, or stupidity. In many of their families there is neither reason for nor tradition of promptness. There is nothing to get up early for; no one hurries.

Many disadvantaged nonwhite children come to have negative feelings about themselves. They believe that they are bound to fail—so many do. They are influenced by the teacher's expectation that they will learn slowly or not at all. When teaching is geared to low expectation of success, many children who have ability become bored, disgusted, and apathetic; make no effort; and withdraw psychologically or even physically, all of which verifies the teacher's prejudgment of them. Instead of punishing the children, the teacher must see what she/he can do to change her/his own attitude and methods. The teacher's admonition "You can't do," and the child's response "I can't" must both be changed. Out of enough success experiences a child learns to say "I can." Success, not failure, provides motivation and releases energy for learning.

What Disadvantaged Children Miss

Perhaps the best way to show what the disadvantaged miss in early life is to describe what most middle-class parents (white and nonwhite) do for their children—very little of which is done in the house of poverty and ignorance.

Middle-class parents talk to and with their children from infancy. Words are taught, repeated, corrected; and the child is rewarded for learning them. By constant feedback from adults and older siblings, the child learns correct ways of putting words together. Conversation is extended, and she/he is encouraged to express her/his thoughts, to tell how she/he feels and what she/he wants to do. Questions are welcomed and answered as fully as possible.

The middle-class child early learns relationships in time and space. Through being directed to look and see, to listen and hear, the child develops audio and visual perceptions. She/he learns to obey and to follow directions (which become increasingly complicated). Skills and patterns of response are further developed by the use of games and puzzles. Competition is encouraged by parents who urge, "See who finishes first," "Try to do better than —," "See who can get the most." The winner is always rewarded with prizes, smiles, and praise.

Most middle-class children very soon begin to own things. They learn to want, take care of, have pride in, and share their own private property as well as to keep hands off what belongs to others. Very early many children receive allowances—money they are taught to spend and encouraged to save which helps them to learn to defer satisfaction of immediate desires in favor of future goals.

By the time most middle-class children are three, parents are asking, "What do you want to be when you grow up?" They encourage ever higher aspirations as the children get older. They frequently point out how, to accomplish their aspirations, the children must behave, especially in school.

Even two-year-olds in most middle-class homes, have pictures to look at in magazines, and a plentiful supply of brightly illustrated children's books accumulates in the home. They see adults reading and want to do so, too. Soon they follow along, associating letters and words with pictures. Older siblings often help, and occasionally by the time children are four, sometimes only three, and often by five, they are ready for if not already reading.

Many middle-class parents take their young children on short and long excursions. They go together on foot, in busses, in cars, on trains and boats and planes, to markets, shops, the town, the zoo, the picture gallery, the park, the movies, and the church. On the way parents converse with children, directing attention to people, places, things, and processes, and answering questions about the how and why, the what and where of life.

It is essential for teachers to know that an IQ test score does not indicate that there is a top limit to any child's learning ability. Moreover, no test now in use adequately measures potentialities. IQ scores are regarded by many psychologists as measures of the child's relative level of development. Projects and studies show that IQ test and other scores rise when undernourished and discouraged children receive enough nourishment and rest, when they feel accepted and of worth, and when they are given specific training in test taking and in the subject matter and skills to be tested.

Psychologists and educators say that *intelligence can be created* through providing experiences and opening the individual to their meaning. The "open person" grows and changes as his experiences increase.

Language

Educators talk about the child's *primary language*. Dr. Frank Riessman says, "[One's primary language] is not to be denied lightly, for it is, in very basic ways one's own self. Asking the disadvantaged child to suppress the language he brings to the learning situation is equivalent to demanding that he suppress his identity."*

It is evident that especially for Black slum children, and certainly for Spanish-speaking children, standard English is a secondary language which, perhaps, must be taught as a second language. When pupils and teacher can exchange synonyms and clarify for each other the meanings of culture-tied words and phrases, lessons in vocabulary building are fun for both. Teachers are responsible, however, for explaining that social circumstances dictate the kind of language considered to be in "good taste." They also must make clear to pupils the degree to which the use of standard English is required to get a job, hold it, and move up the ladder of success. This can be done by directing attention to the English used by people the children meet and talk to when they go on trips to factories, industries, and offices, and by the public speakers and others on radio and TV.

At all grade levels and in all subject areas, teachers must assume responsibility for teaching phonics, word analysis, spelling, and comprehension. No matter what the subject and grade level may be, teachers must accept the idea that they must teach whatever a child needs to know to get on with the classroom work.

Time and Hope

Psychologists and sociologists tell us that poverty-stricken people are of necessity oriented to the here and now. They live (or try to) from day to day, dominated by fear and insecurity. Because they have no hope for future achievement or for eventual security, they see no reason for patterns of

---

*Quoted from Riessman, Frank, *The Culturally Deprived Child.* New York: Harper & Row, 1962.

behavior directed toward the future. A teacher who does not understand this may misjudge a child's inability to forego immediate satisfactions in favor of future goals. A simple example of this is children who eat whatever they may have whenever they want to. They devour lunch as soon as they arrive in class with never a thought about what they will do when lunchtime comes.

How, in the face of the disorganized, disoriented lives of children whose families have little or no hope for the future, can the school help these children to conceive of the role time plays in upward mobility? Studies of poverty-stricken people in rural and urban depressed areas show that their lack of motivation stems largely from hopelessness. One way the school can provide experiences from which pupils, if not their parents, may gather hope and begin to direct their lives toward the future is for teachers in upper elementary grades through senior high school to take their classes on trips to business establishments, factories, industrial plants, cultural facilities, educational establishments, and governmental offices where they can see members of their groups at work at all levels. On such trips minority group workers, supervisors, and executives should be asked to tell the children about their own backgrounds, their struggles and successes. When trips are not possible, successful minority group adults can be brought into the schools to address assemblies, talk to classroom groups, and meet with individuals who need their guidance and inspiration. In this way children learn at first hand that more and more employment doors are opening to people like themselves, and that success depends upon becoming qualified.

WHAT TEACHERS CAN DO FOR SIXES AND SEVENS

Experience and research projects indicate that for first-grade disadvantaged children who did not go to nursery school, or kindergarten, teachers should probably abandon their regular beginning procedures and courses of study, substituting for them many of the teaching-learning activities the children missed at home or in preschool projects. Instead of teaching them to sit still and not talk, the teacher is urged to encourage them to move freely, to engage in free and joyous play, and to freely express their thoughts, feelings, reactions, and intentions. The children need to learn how to ask and answer questions.

Teachers are also told to make language development their main objective and to provide new experiences with things, places, and people, so that concepts are developed along with word symbols. Fairy stories, nursery rhymes, and songs which the children want to hear over and over, to save time and energy, can be recorded on discs or tape and individual earphones provided.

Even at six or seven, some severely disadvantaged children may not know their own names (or much else about themselves) if they are not used to hearing and answering to their names. Songs and games help; so do mirrors and photographs. School probably provides these children their first opportunities to dress up and play many roles, which helps them to differentiate between themselves and others. Play-acting will give them a chance to express their feelings about themselves and others. Role playing produces understanding of people, especially adults.

Experience indicates that many disadvantaged children need specific training in perceiving time, space, and size relationships and in learning the words and phrases which describe them. Experiences with things, places, and people; with doing, hearing, and seeing; and with handling and using materials will be required before children learn to identify, name, compare, differentiate, abstract common characteristics, generalize, and categorize. Mass instruction is not usually successful in accomplishing these learnings. Teachers need aides and semiprofessionals to help them work with individuals and small groups.

A child cannot avoid making mistakes, but mistakes should be regarded and used as learning experiences. In every situation the teacher should emphasize and praise whatever the child does right. Every success should be recognized by the teacher, received with joy, and rewarded in some way. These are general methods of relating to children in the classroom which are especially important in teaching the disadvantaged. Above all, disadvantaged children, even more than others, need to know that the teacher accepts them, likes them, and wants them in the room.

WHAT TEACHERS CAN DO FOR 8- TO 11-YEAR-OLDS

Too many eight-year-old children are already accustomed to failure and neglect, convinced that they cannot learn to read and that no one cares whether or not they do. In some, patterns of aggression, withdrawal, and psychosomatic illness are becoming evident. The unsatisfied need for adult approval is already turning them toward the peer group, loyalty to which may motivate hostility and resistance to the demands, restrictions, and authority of the school.

Especially in elementary and in desegregated secondary schools, the absence of minority-group male teachers and counselors means that boys have few if any male models whose values and behavior they might want to accept and copy. Boys often seek models in the "successful" and possibly delinquent older youths of the neighborhood. To offset this lack, it is suggested that teachers bring in for assembly programs and interviews, or to talk to classroom groups, minority group adults and college youth who, by their personalities, work, and life stories, can inspire the pupils with ambition and hope.

In grades 3, 4, and 5 very special individualized efforts must be made to reach and teach children who have not yet learned to read. Early research on reading underachievement revealed that very often the real causes of the difficulty were emotional problems caused by bad human relations at home and in school. It is also becoming clear that when children find no similarity between the people and situations pictured in the reading books and themselves and their lives, or when the content of the books is too trivial, they tend to reject them and may even refuse to learn to read.

Teachers find that the experience method used in primary grades can also be successful in the middle grades, if it is adapted to the maturity level of the pupils. In some classrooms, instead of the teacher's writing one chart from pupils' dictation on their return from a field trip, each pupil writes his own "book." Children usually enjoy writing books about themselves and their own experiences and sharing them with the group. These can be used instead of primers, which are entirely unsuitable and insult the intelligence of 8- to 11-year-olds.

In many cases, not enough training in audio and visual perception and in pronunciation has been provided in the primary grades. In the middle grades, therefore, many pupils do not recognize or sound the basic letters and letter combinations, so teaching and practicing phonics must continue to occupy portions of the school day. Pupil pairs and teams organized and trained for drill activities are used successfully. The children often make their own flash cards, illustrating them with drawings or pictures clipped from magazines. Concentrated work on word recognition and analysis, comprehension, and use of new words in sentences is indicated for most pupils.

Drill on memorizing number combinations will be of little value for children who have missed the meaning of the basic arithmetical processes. Concrete materials used in primary grades should continue to be available so that individual children can work with them until they understand what addition, subtraction, multiplication, division, and fractions really mean. Number symbols cannot be used successfully until the concept of number has been developed.

There is danger in the middle grades that so-called basic education will replace all the other subjects. The teacher must also plan learning experiences for all the children, whether or not they can read, which will open them to their natural environment, to people, places, and things as well as to organized social life. Science, social studies, art, music, practical arts, hygiene, and physical health and fitness can be learned without books. Of course, many and varied pictures and books to supplement direct learning experiences should be accessible at all times to those who can read. The nonreader also should be allowed to have them in hand so as to follow along when teacher or classmates read aloud.

WHAT JUNIOR HIGH SCHOOL TEACHERS CAN DO FOR DISADVANTAGED ADOLESCENTS

For the disadvantaged, as for all other early adolescents, the junior high school years are a time of physical growth and emotional rebellion. Teachers should, therefore, not expect these young people to be as orderly and quiet, or as docilely obedient and willing to conform to regimentation, as little children may be. Nevertheless, freedom should not become license, nor should teachers abdicate their responsibilities for maintaining conditions that enable them to fulfill their teaching responsibilities. They should, however, give the pupils the chance to participate in setting up the limits to behavior in the classroom and in determining the consequences for infractions (but not to administer punishments). Furthermore, units of work in subject areas are more likely to arouse interest and hold attention when pupils participate in their planning. They will be more successful if they include or originate in the questions pupils ask and the problems on which they want to work as well as needs identified by the teacher. Lectures should be replaced by small-group work and individual projects as emphasis shifts from teaching to learning. Objectives should include development of leadership skills; individual and group controls; and the ability to evaluate self, process, and product. The importance of fact should be stressed, and skill should be developed in gathering information from people, places, things, radio, television, and films as well as from the printed word in books, magazines, and newspapers. The individual should be permitted to express what she/he has learned in any way that fits her/his abilities. Paintings, posters, charts, graphs, maps, models, mock-ups, collections, and oral reports should be encouraged and received with warmth and praise equal to that given for written reports.

Teachers of all subjects are urged to become reading teachers, accepting responsibility for teaching pupils to recognize, spell, pronounce, use, and read the material needed in their classrooms. Installation of language laboratories requires in-service education of teachers. Programmed arithmetic and language study books and machines, and science kits, should be available to supplement teachers' presentations but not to replace the teacher-pupil relationship so important to these children. Tape recorders help in speech correction and language development.

Adolescence is a time of searching for identity, for warm relationships, and for the meaning of organized life. Political ideologies must therefore be openly and factually discussed in social studies classrooms. Television and radio broadcasts are natural discussion starters. In all of this work, efforts should be made to distinguish facts from opinion, rumor, gossip, and propaganda.

WHAT SENIOR HIGH SCHOOL TEACHERS CAN DO

Many students lack a personal relationship with even one teacher. They are sure no one really cares whether or not they learn, whether or not they attend, whether or not they graduate.

As the result of years of frustration, failure, and often humiliation, many have acquired deeply ingrained feelings of inferiority and hopelessness. They believe teachers expect them to do poor work and behave badly, and so they see no reason to try. Many already have more schooling than their adults, who give them little encouragement to remain in school.

Because most teachers make little attempt to discover student interests and needs, the students believe that teachers are content to teach only what is in the books or what they are interested in. They resent the lack of connection between the course content and the realities of the life they lead outside of school.

Those who, through the grades, were reclassified by chronological age rather than achievement and whose inability to read was ignored are doomed to failure in subjects for which textbooks are the main teaching instrument.

Can the teachers change the senior high school pattern for such students? Unless they do, many will drop out, and some of those who stay will eventually land on society's "scrap heap."

Much is being done to discover "academically able," but disadvantaged, students. Tutoring in reading by college students, classmates, or adults which provides a one-to-one relationship is helping many. Teachers say the recognition and reinforcement which a student experiences when she/he is assigned to teach a nonreader result in raising her/his own reading level as well as that of the pupil being taught.

High school girls and boys will soon be parents, yet most schools are doing little if anything to prepare them. School can and should give disadvantaged youth insight into what parents must supply their children to break the cycle of poverty, unemployment, dependency, and despair. Social workers can be brought in to provide realistic appraisals of slum life and to help students improve their own living conditions. If the school opens cultural activities to these students, they, as parents in turn, will be more likely to provide similar cultural opportunities for their children. Reports of the gains made in adequately financed programs are encouraging.

The senior high school students' acute need for money can be met in some measure by increasing the number of work-study programs. Community action groups can be called upon to provide some money to pay students for doing some jobs in school, including tutoring younger children. Understanding and cooperative teachers and counselors need to increase their efforts to help students get jobs, solve their work problems, and develop the personality traits required for success in the working world.

Unless school personnel now accept responsibility for developing the potentialities of disadvantaged adolescents, for making "somebodies" out of young people who according to their own self-evaluation are "nobodies," the next decade will see mounting rather than decreasing numbers of unemployable and dependent adults. Control of crime, alcoholism, drug addiction, and mental illness, already difficult, may overwhelm the resources of the large cities. The nation looks to the schools for leadership in saving and developing our most valuable resources—the youth.

The Sensory Environment: A Building Block to Learning

by G. F. McVey

In order to create an environment that will have a positive effect on the health and physical development as well as the academic performance of their students, classroom teachers need to understand the effects of the many sensory stimuli arising in the classroom. Traditionally, teachers have depended upon their own commonsense observations of how sensory stimuli work in the learning environment. Some of the research findings included in this report confirm such observations; other findings provide new information and insights.

UNITY OF THE SENSES

Stimuli can either facilitate or inhibit perception. The senses are functionally linked, and stimulation of one affects the sensibility of all the others. Thus, a moderate input of sound or light improves sensory reception, while an excessive input inhibits or retards it. Research has shown how disagreeable odors retard motor performance and vision, and how moderate lighting in a room makes hearing and tactile discrimination easier.

The exact nature of this interplay between the senses is still uncertain, and the processes by which it occurs are still vague. One possible explanation is that the nerve fibers that handle sensory information in the brain are in close proximity and are not insulated from each other; stimulation of one fiber can be conducted to a neighboring fiber. If this accessory stimulation is moderate, it may lower the threshold on the second fiber, facilitating the transmission of other stimuli. If the accessory stimulation is excessive, it may raise the threshold, inhibiting the reception of incoming signals.

The classroom teacher can safely act on the principle that moderate stimulation of one sense will facilitate the reception of information through the others, and that excessive stimulation will inhibit this process.

While the most common stimuli found in the classroom are energy forms—light, sound, heat, vibration, etc.—other factors such as time of day, seating arrangements, novelty, colors, other classmates, and, of course, the teacher are also important environmental stimuli. In fact, any physical element or situation in the classroom which causes a change in the human organism, no matter how small, can be considered a stimulus.

Reactions to Stimuli

Generally speaking, there are three gross reactions to stimuli: orientation, adaption, and defense. It is the orientation reaction, according to the Russian physiologist Pavlov, which brings about the immediate response in human beings and animals to changes in the world around them. When there is a moderate but significant change in some environmental stimulus, the organism immediately orients its appropriate receptor toward the change, with the intention of making full investigation of it.

The orientation response is one of attention or inquisitiveness. In the classroom, a light suddenly turned on or a book falling from a desk and striking the floor evokes this type of response. The orientation response includes such basic physical reactions as increased sensitivity of the senses and orientation toward the stimulus source, and such specific reactions as an increase in general muscle tonus and brain electrostimulation, greater depth of respiration, and slower heart rate. All of these responses tend to raise the level of a student's readiness to perform physical and mental tasks.

A teacher can take advantage of the orientation reflex to underscore important points in lesson presentations. By striking the chalkboard with a pointer she/he can draw attention to those words and sentences that are most important. In visual displays the students' attention can be captured and maintained to key areas by the use of brighter chalk, color, or even light.

If the stimulus is weak or moderate, the initial orientation response is followed by an adaptive reaction. For example, when illumination is decreased, adaptive reactions include pupil dilation, which increases light influx, and dark adaptation, which increases retinal sensitivity. Adaptive reactions to an increase in illumination include pupil contraction, which decreases light influx, and light adaption, which decreases retinal sensitivity.

When a stimulus is of an excessive magnitude, defensive reactions occur. The subject reacts in the extreme by turning away from the stimulus, by aggressively approaching it with the intention of terminating it, or sometimes by "freezing" in place. Defensive reactions can be observed when an excessively bright light is turned on or a sudden loud noise occurs. If the stimulus continues, after a while the subject will adapt to it, but at the cost of decreased sensitivity (e.g., a temporary hearing loss) or an expenditure of additional energy.

Quite often a teacher unknowingly sets up perceptual conflict by directing students to view a classroom television set or some other informational display set up adjacent to a glaring luminaire or exposed window. Here the students' autonomic defensive mechanism directs them to turn away from the excessively bright light at the same time that their classroom task is to attend to the visual presentation.

It is important for the teacher to be able to predict the basic responses of students to stimuli of different magnitudes in order to be able to coordinate these in a way that will aid learning and physical comfort. She/he should strive to evoke the orientation reaction and to eliminate defensive reactions in students. The teacher as manager of the classroom environment should not allow conflicts between task and surroundings to occur.

THE VISUAL LEARNING ENVIRONMENT

Although the composite perception of all the senses is most important, and vision is but one avenue of information, it is generally agreed that most learning comes through the sense of vision.

Viewing Distances

We have the ability to perceive objects over an extremely wide visual field of approximately 200 degrees. However, of this area only a narrow field of 30 degrees offers a high degree of visual acuity. It is estimated that approximately 70 percent of all vision takes place within this narrow field. Consequently, if we want an object or display, such as a projection screen, to be viewed with relative accuracy, it should be of such a size or at such a distance as to fall within this 30-degree cone of the viewer's vision.

When computed in image widths, the cone of critical vision turns out to have a length of 2W—that is, two times the width of the display. This distance has become the universally accepted *minimum* distance for viewing most displays when detection of information is important, as in classroom movies, slides, and filmstrips. For example, with a projection screen 4 feet wide, the minimum viewing distance would be 2 x 4 feet, or 8 feet. The only medium that deviates from the 2W rule is television. Here most specialists recommend a 4W minimum viewing distance, because at distances less than 4W the scan lines of the image are too prominent and thus distracting.

The *optimum* viewing distance for the detection of information in the visual field is 6¼W. Therefore, for a TV monitor 19 inches wide, the optimum viewing distance would be 6¼ x 19 inches, or 119 inches (approximately ten feet). At this distance, the eye takes in the whole image, rather than concentrating on a particular section.

Viewing Angles

As a viewer moves away from the axis perpendicular to a displayed image, she/he experiences an increasing amount of distortion because a flat surface is being viewed from a more and more oblique angle. Viewing locations up to a point 45 degrees from the outside of the screen will produce images with an acceptable amount of distortion. Beyond this angle, viewing is excessively distorted, and the legibility of words and the identifiability of charts are adversely affected.

Excessive angles of elevation tend to arise in the classroom where the teacher, attempting to place the display or TV or projector screen high enough for students in the back to see, overcompensates and places it too high, causing students in the front rows to view up at fatiguing angles. Excessive angles of depression, on the other hand, are likely to be present in auditoriums where seating is stepped or inclined drastically from the front to the back rows.

Lighting

Lighting is perhaps the most important sensory factor to be considered in the learning environment. Current research indicates that a lighting level somewhere between 30 and 50 footcandles is adequate for the comfortable and effective completion of most visual tasks. Most fluorescent fixtures found in the classroom provide more than enough light for most learning tasks.

Brightness-Contrast Ratio

The quality and placement of light are of major significance; quantity is a secondary factor, as long as minimum acceptable levels are maintained. One of the most important factors in classroom lighting is the brightness-contrast ratio (BCR)—the ratio of the brightness of the central task area to the brightness of the "surround" or background. In order to guarantee depth perception in three dimensions, contour detection, and visual comfort, the BCR should be somewhere between a minimum of 2.5 to 1 and a maximum of 10 to 1. The optimum BCR is 3 to 1, the standard adopted by the illuminating Engineering Society.

One does not need elaborate measuring devices to set up BCR's that are approximately correct. Subjective judgment works fairly well. It is important that a proper BCR be maintained when using visual aids, for it will promote both visual comfort and seeing accuracy. Since different visual aids vary in their light output, classroom lighting should be varied also. A general principle to remember is that all visual aids should be displayed in rooms dark enough so that image details and colors are accurately rendered, but no darker.

Color

Color is a vital part of most people's lives. It can change moods and judgments of size, weight, and distance, induce body tonus, and in general enhance the quality of life.

Many of our psychophysical responses to color have been attributed to the phenomenon known as chromatic aberration. The human eye is not color-corrected, meaning that it does not focus light of different colors at the same point. In order to bring colors into focus, the lens of the eye must vary its shape. For example, the eye projects violet and blue in front of the retina, the lens flattens, and the result is that these colors appear to recede. Red and orange, on the other hand, are projected somewhere behind the retina; the lens grows convex, with the result that those colors appear to be approaching. An object either colored or illuminated by the color blue will thus appear to be farther away and smaller than a red, orange, or even yellow object.

Chromatic aberration is probably the physiological basis for the psychological effects of colors, i.e., for our perception of colors as "warm" and "stimulating" or "cool" and "relaxing." Many color specialists recommend that rooms scheduled to be action-oriented be decorated in the warmer colors (yellow, orange, red), and those planned for quiet activities in the cooler colors (green, blue).

Many elementary school teachers intuitively make use of the effects of chromatic aberration by wearing bright and colorful clothes on days when they plan to introduce new and difficult lessons. Visual displays such as slides, bulletin boards, and dioramas can also make good use of the psychospatial effects of colors by highlighting the most important elements with red and orange and adding depth to the backgrounds with blue.

THE ACOUSTICAL LEARNING ENVIRONMENT

Noise has been universally defined as unwanted sound. Whether a sound is noise or not is a subjective judgment determined by the meaning the sound has for an individual and by the situation in which it occurs. A school bell signaling the start of recess may be perceived by many students as a sign of relief from a tedious morning. But the same bell terminating an all-too-brief exam period will be perceived as an intrusive, frustrating noise.

Even when students are studying quietly there is ambient sound present in the classroom. This background sound is created by many things: the flow of air from the air exchange system, the mechanical sound of the fans that move this air, the buzzing of light filaments and fluorescent light ballasts, the vibration of the electric clock, and the sounds intruding from the class next door. Such background noise is accepted as a desirable component of the classroom as long continuous background noise. If a classroom were free of all background noise students could literally hear themselves think. They would be constantly distracted by the sound of their own breathing and heartbeat, let alone the movements of the students around them.

Effects of Excessive Noise

Today the problem of noise pollution within the classroom caused by external sources such as traffic, construction, and aircraft has reached grave proportions. Excessive noise is inimical to the "listening" process, that is, to the psychological process by which one comprehends verbal information, as well as to the "hearing" process, which is the physiological process of receiving meaningless sound. When we consider that the average person spends 45 percent of her/his waking hours in some listening-related task, the problem of noise and communication becomes apparent. Excessive noise has also been shown to have an adverse effect on reading comprehension and on retention, recall, and recognition of materials.

Background Music

In recent years there have been many attempts to use music as background sound for various school tasks. The success or failure of such attempts has depended upon the nature of the music and the nature of the task. While nonfamiliar music, especially if it has few major frequency and volume shifts, can help many students concentrate on their work, familiar music can be an informational distraction. The rhythm of the music is most important. If it does not match the rhythm of the work task (typing, handwriting, or whatever), it can cause a decrement in the students' performance.

Music, in general, tends to speed up the fundamental physiological processes and to raise the level of body tonus. Because it also tends to increase muscle endurance, music can reduce or delay the fatigue associated with a physical work task.

THE THERMAL LEARNING ENVIRONMENT

Illumination and sound are the chief sensory factors affecting information display and transmission in the classroom, but other sensory factors affect the physical comfort and energy consumption that accompany study and work. Four of these factors come under the general heading of the thermal environment: air temperature, radiant temperature, humidity, and air movement. These are interrelated in such a way that each affects the contribution of the others to the resultant comfort level.

The job of the thermal environment is to allow the human body to maintain its deep body temperature—98.6*—while performing its tasks. A human being can be thought of as a furnace; the food she/he eats is the fuel. Every activity the "furnace" engages in, whether primarily mental, such as problem solving, or muscular, such as athletics, consumes energy supplied initially by food intake. It is estimated that a child seated at a desk working at a mental problem uses more than twice as much energy as she/he does when asleep. When a task requires much energy, the environment must absorb the heat by-product that is generated. When a task requires little energy, the environment must provide heat at a level that helps the body to perform in comfort.

CLASSROOM SPACE AND FUNITURE

Anthropologists tell us that every organism has an intuitive and learned concept of physical space and its interrelationship with it. This sense of space is closely related to the sense of territoriality—the invisible set of spatial limits that one sets up around oneself and allows to be entered only under specific circumstances. A leading anthropologist has divided this envelope of "personal space" into four major distance categories: intimate (6 to 18 inches), personal (1½ to 4 feet), social (4 to 12 feet), and public (12 feet or more). He has also identified the kinds of behavior we can expect to occur when these spaces are not respected.

------

*This is the mean, with approximate lower and upper limits of 97 degrees and 99 degrees Fahrenheit.

Students and teachers alike are continually establishing and reestablishing their concepts of personal space and territoriality. Young children in particular try to zone off areas they can call their own. It is no wonder that when these personal spaces are violated—as in the overcrowded class-room—students tend to become less productive and to lose their sense of identity.

In general, classroom spaces can be classified as those that tend to keep students apart and those that tend to bring them together. Students need to have both types of space available to them: spaces where they can be alone with their thoughts and imagination, as well as spaces that help them interact with others. Today's modern schools include both types of spaces. Carrels and library reading rooms tend to separate students, while playgrounds and small conference classrooms tend to bring them together.

Innovations in Classroom Design

It is encouraging to note that a number of today's newer schools have been designed around the modular program and thus have classrooms of different sizes and shapes where a variety of interaction patterns can be effectively set up. The large multiclassroom represents another attempt to use space as an instructional element. Its proponents argue that the large open space adds a sense of freedom and informality to the learning situation and gives increased versatility to the instructional program. This could very well be true, but the success or failure of the multiclassroom, as of other innova-tions, depends heavily upon teacher attitude. The multi-classroom has been successful in schools where the teachers wanted it. Where it has failed, teacher attitude was negative; teachers complained of the noise, the reduction of visual privacy, and the challenge to their autonomy.

Here we see an example of the conflict between a teach-er's concept of "personal space" and the spatial arrangement some educational planner thinks is necessary for a particular instructional program. Some teachers and students have gone so far as to partition off their class space with bookcases, desks, portable chalkboards, and the like, in an effort to achieve a sense of territoriality. Fortunately, much of the new educational thinking is sensitive to these and related problems. Attention is being given to the design of flexible spaces which will provide for the territorial needs of students and faculty, and efforts are being made to reeducate teachers to perceive these flexible spaces not as invasions of their dominions, but as opportunities for the dynamic expansion of their instructional programs.

CONCLUSION

The classroom is not just a shelter the teacher and her/ his students have to live with, but rather an educational tool that can be manipulated in many ways. Through proper management of the sensory factors inherent in the classroom environment, teachers can improve the comfort, development, and academic performance of their students. We have suggested a number of guidelines drawn from reasearch findings. However, it is possible that by rigidly following optimum standards and specifications without providing the element of variation, teachers and school planners risk producing a static environment which can by its very nature have adverse effects. Rather, the learning environment should provide stimuli that continuously vary within permissible parameters. The classroom should be a place of diversity, a place where mental and physical growth and development can proceed unimpeded by environmental constraints.

Listening: A Particular Sensory Concern

by Stanford E. Taylor

Listening, an act accepted by children and adults as second nature, is rapidly becoming one of our newest and most intriguing educational frontiers. Most teachers of the primary grades are aware of the children who cannot discriminate well among the sounds of our language and who, therefore, cannot take full advantage of instruction in phonetic analysis. Likewise, the intermediate-grade teacher is all too familiar with children who cannot or do not follow directions without numerous repetitions and who cannot listen analytically or critically.

This condition is not surprising when one considers the negligible amount of instruction provided in listening, the lack of a sequential developmental listening program in most schools, and the inherent complexity of the listening act.

FROM A SOUND TO MEANING

Listening starts with the speaker who utters sounds at a certain level of loudness, from a certain distance, with a particular manner of enunciation. Although the listener is unaware of the process, she/he does not receive a word instantly but rather accumulates sound, receiving a word over a brief but measurable interval of time.

During the third of a second it takes to hear a syllable, or during the several seconds it takes to listen to an idea, many factors affect the translation of sound into meaning. Gaining a clearer understanding of these factors is an important first step for any teacher who wants to improve listening abilities.

While the total act of receiving auditory communication is generally referred to as "listening," it may be clearer to think of this act in three distinguishable stages: hearing, listening, and auding.

Hearing is used to designate the process by which speech sounds in the form of sound waves are received and modified by the ear.

Listening refers to the process of becoming aware of sound sequences. In listening to speech, the person first

104

identifies the component sounds and then recognizes sound sequences as known words through the avenues of auditory analysis, mental reorganization, and/or association of meaning.

Auding refers to the process by which the continuous flow of words is translated into meaning. Auding involves one or more avenues of thought—indexing, making comparisons, noting sequence, forming sensory impressions, and appreciating.

FACTORS WHICH INFLUENCE HEARING

A fundamental consideration in the hearing stage is the student's ability to receive speech sounds accurately in daily communication situations, which normally involve a certain amount of background noise and sometimes conflicting conversations. The factors which must be considered are auditory acuity, masking, fatigue, and binaural consideration.

Auditory Acuity

Once sound enters the ear of a listener, the first factor to affect her/his hearing of sound is auditory acuity, or the physical response of the ear to sound vibrations. Auditory acuity may be thought of as the ability to respond to various frequencies (tones) at various intensities (levels of loudness).

When hearing is tested, a person's ability to hear is checked across the entire speech frequency range. A person is said to have a hearing loss when she/he requires more than the normal amount of volume in order to hear sounds of certain frequencies.

Masking

The next factor to influence hearing is masking, a condition in which the message being listened to is made less audible by the superimposition of other sounds, for sounds of the same frequency can alter one another. In the classroom, background noise and, most certainly, nearby conversation can have the effect of masking the voice being listened to.

Auditory Fatigue

Auditory fatigue may be thought of as a temporary hearing loss. Continuous or repeated exposure to sounds of certain frequencies can have the effect of reducing the listener's ability to hear those frequencies in subsequent exposures. A monotonous tone or a droning voice will have the effect of inducing auditory fatigue, for sounds within the speech range are the most likely to produce fatigue.

Binaural Considerations

Similar to the stereopsis (depth perception) produced by binocular vision is the localizing effect of binaural hearing. Localizing refers to the listener's ability to place a sound source or judge its distance and direction. Such judgments are based on the intensity of the sound arriving at each ear and on the difference in the time it takes for the sound to reach each ear.

Binaural hearing also enables the listener to keep separate two or more sound sources. When in the presence of two or more conversations, the average listener should find it possible to direct her/his attention to one speaker or conversation, suppressing the others, and to shift attention from one to another. Being able to separate the sound sources helps listeners to keep their messages "straight." Recent studies have shown that less capable listeners encounter greater difficulty in keeping their messages straight.

FACTORS WHICH INFLUENCE LISTENING

Beyond the factors which influence hearing are those that affect one's awareness of speech sounds or speech patterns and determine the way in which one identifies and recognizes sounds as words.

Attention and Concentration

Among the first factors to be considered are attention and concentration. Attention may be thought of as the directing of awareness; concentration, as a sustaining of attention. Some researchers have gone so far as to suggest that listening is little more than bringing attention and concentration to bear on an auditory stimulus. But what enables a person to attend and concentrate? Among the important considerations are the general mental and physical well being of the listener, her/his acquired attitudes toward listening and learning, and her/his learned ability to focus attention.

To sustain attention, other conditions are necessary. The content must be such that it can be "taken in stride," for if the message is too difficult in relation to the listener's ability to assimilate or manipulate ideas, her/his attention may wane, or she/he may take refuge in selective listening to escape from what has been referred to as "information input overload." On the other hand, the content must be challenging, for if the message is too simple, the listener will soon find relief by taking mental excursions.

Auditory Analysis

When using auditory analysis, the listener is very conscious of the characteristics of the sound. She/he relies heavily on *auditory* discrimination when the aural message is less meaningful or meaningless. She/he compares the sounds heard with other familiar sounds, generally noting likenesses and differences. Though unaware of doing so, the listener is responding to changes in frequency (pitch or tone), intensity (volume), periodicity (rhythm), and the manner in which these changes take place.

Mental Reorganization

A second means of identification and recognition is that of mental reorganization, a process that is typically used with less meaningful material. In using mental reorganization listeners employ a system that will aid retention. For example, they may syllabify a word or name, pronouncing it to themselves. When presented with a long series of numbers or letters, the listener will attempt to think of them in groups of two, three, or four elements.

Association of Meaning

Words are also identified and recognized because of their meanings and uses. They are more easily apprehended when they are part of predictable and meaningful speech. The extent to which meaning is associated is dependent first on the listener's *experience and background* and secondly on her/his ability to use aural *context* clues. Listeners must be able to anticipate wording as they listen and to confirm or correct in retrospect as they continue to listen. They must be able to "listen between the words" and capitalize on the speaker's manner of delivery, noting tone and the mood created, responding to phrasing and emphasis on certain words, and realizing the way in which the speaker organizes ideas.

Rate of Input

Once the listener has identified a sound or recognized a sound sequence as a familiar word, the next factor to be considered is rate of input, for listening is a continuous act and must be thought of in terms of sound units received per unit of time—syllables per second, or words per minute. Rate studies have been conducted in which the pause time between words was varied, in which the speaker varied the rate of delivery, and in which recorded speech was compressed mechanically.

In general, most of the studies showed that the listener preferred a speaking rate between 150 and 175 words per minute. If, however, the content was judged difficult by the listener, a slower rate of delivery was preferred.

Unrelated Associations

It is important to realize that words used in speech may call forth, in addition to the intended meaning, a host of unrelated associations which may distract from or alter communication. The listener may react emotionally, either positively or negatively, to a particular word or phrase to the extent that a message is completely misinterpreted because of the presence of that word or phrase.

FACTORS WHICH INFLUENCE AUDING

As each word is recognized it is added to, and becomes part of, the larger spoken message. As the listener assimilates the continuous flow of words, she/he must aud, i.e., respond with understanding or feeling. In auding, the listener brings into play all of her/his *experience and background* and the thinking skills that allow her/him to index, make comparisons, note sequence, react by forming sensory impressions, or appreciate what is heard.

Listeners are able to aud by using the surplus thinking time that is usually available during listening. Even in the primary grades, a teacher will sense the ability of many children to "think ahead" of a speaker. In the case of more mature listeners, the difference between listening rate and thinking rate may be as great as three or four hundred words per minute.

Thinking skills used during the auding act are quite similar to those employed during reading, writing, and speaking. It is for this reason that reading and listening measurements involving these common attributes correlate highly and that training in these skills through listening activities produces a gain in both reading and listening.

LISTENING, READING, INTELLIGENCE, AND SCHOLASTIC ABILITY

Listening and reading are both receptive communication acts, as opposed to speaking and writing, which are expressive acts. Listening and reading differ primarily in the manner in which an individual receives and recognizes words; they are alike because the individual brings to both the same experience background and employs many of the same thinking skills in each. How do these similarities and differences affect the student's use of listening and reading?

In the primary and intermediate grades, listening abilities are more advanced than reading skills for students who are average in intelligence and scholastic ability. Children in this age range prefer to listen rather than read, when offered a choice. Listening is preferred because it is a more "usual" act, one in which the student has had many years of experience. Reading, on the other hand, is a slower and less efficient process both in terms of word recognition and rate of thinking. As a result, listening usually makes possible better comprehension and retention than does reading.

Listening and reading reach equivalence in both word recognition rate and in word-per-minute rate during the early part of sixth grade. Not until the latter part of sixth grade or seventh grade, however, does reading appear to gain sufficient efficiency to cause it to be preferred over the usual act of listening in many learning situations.

During sixth or seventh grade, listening is preferred when the content is "easy," while reading is preferred when the content is judged difficult. The explanation for this probably lies in the fact that listening is paced by a speaker, who usually presents ideas in a steady, relatively uninterrupted manner; in reading, the students pace themselves, can double-check and reread, and can pause and reflect when necessary.

Below the sixth or seventh grade, individual students will tend to prefer reading as soon as their reading proficiency reaches or exceeds the level of their listening proficiency. If their reading development is slow, they will continue to rely most heavily on listening beyond the seventh grade.

Above grade 7, there is a distinct preference for reading over listening in most learning situations, and better retention results from reading. With each passing year reading proficiency increases, and the complexity of the material to be learned likewise increases. These factors encourage an ever greater preference for reading.

In general, less competent students, those judged to be less intelligent and scholastically below average, show a marked preference for listening over reading in most learning situations and do retain more from listening. Slower students depend on the special attributes of listening for much of their understanding. In listening, they are assisted in interpreting content by the phrasing and expression of the speaker, while in reading they must construct their own linguistic units in order to realize meaning.

CAN LISTENING BE TAUGHT?

Just as there is a growing awareness of the importance of listening, there has also been an increase in the number of studies indicating that listening skills can be taught and that listening ability does improve substantially when specific instruction is provided. In every study reported in which listening instruction had been given, pronounced gains were made in listening and often in allied communication skills as well.

Because learning is so dependent on listening, because most students are not accomplished listeners, a developmental listening improvement program is needed in most schools. In instituting such a program, a number of factors must be considered.

Improving conditions that affect hearing

Although the percentage of students that is likely to be handicapped by hearing losses is relatively small, it is desirable to have the hearing of all students checked with an audiometer. If a student's average hearing loss is less than 20 decibels, changing her/his seat in a class may be sufficient. Students with a loss greater than 20 decibels in the speech frequencies may require special training in auditory discrimination. While this training cannot improve hearing as such, it can help the student to make better use of the auditory cues she/he does hear. If a hearing loss is 35 decibels or more, a special hearing aid will probably prove necessary.

Creating the Proper Listening Climate

Many improvements can be made in listening by careful consideration of the quality of the listening climate. It is important to realize that in many classrooms, the teacher provides the majority of the listening climate. With this in mind, the teacher should carefully appraise the amount of time students are expected to listen during each school day. In taking stock, most teachers are amazed to find that students are expected to listen during the greater portion of the school day.

Improving Listening Attitudes

Most students have already formed certain attitudes toward listening as a result of experiences in school and at home. To many, listening is simply "getting told," and this has not always been a pleasant experience. As a consequence, they often seek refuge in not listening, or listening in a passive manner, knowing that almost everything that is truly important will be repeated.

With younger children, changing the listening climate and providing activities that place a premium on listening carefully and attentively will produce the desired changes in attitude. With older students, however, the teacher may find it advisable to employ a number of specific approaches in order to change attitudes toward listening.

Teaching Listening as a Tool for Learning

Much improvement can be effected by continued stress on the use of good listening in all daily learning stituations. Students should be made aware of using listening as a tool of learning. Likewise, the teacher should carry out a directed listening activity whenever presenting subject-area content orally. Whenever directions are given orally, the "once only" rule should be observed, so that a value is placed on the speaker's and the listener's time. When students are asked to listen appreciatively, guidance should be provided in how to listen and for what to listen.

Providing Planned Instruction in Certain
Listening Skills

Although a certain amount of growth in listening will result from attention to listening in daily instruction and an improved listening climate, greater growth will be achieved when a planned program of listening training is also provided.

Such a program would start with an appraisal of the students' existing listening skills, using formal or informal measurements. Informal testing might take the form of an informal listening and auding inventory, through which the teacher would attempt to evaluate such factors as students' auditory discrimination, their individual abilities to use context in predicting words and ideas, and to use the various auding skills with content suitable for their level and to the extent that they can learn satisfactorily in the types of situations they encounter in daily classroom work.

A systematic and regularly scheduled training program is necessary to introduce the needed skills and abilities and to provide the amount of practice that is necessary to assure mastery of these skills and abilities.

At present, concern about listening is growing, and the number of studies related to the component skills of listening, listening instruction, and listening in relation to other factors is mounting. But the critical step is still to be taken—that of incorporating developmental listening instruction into the school curriculum.

What is needed is a systematic listening program that will develop flexible listeners, persons who are both effective and efficient in a wide range of listening situations. They are effective because they have at their command the insights and the specific skills with which to approach each listening situation. They are efficient because they possess the auditory sensitivity and the·functional facility that permit them to carry out listening tasks with a minimum expenditure of time and energy.

Media: A Current and Future Environment

by Gerald M. Torkelson

TYPES OF MEDIA

The immediate society from which the learner comes tends to be her/his real world. Might it not be natural to expect that a generation of learners who have "teethed" on television, Saturday movies, pictorial magazines, roadside advertising, and the use of pictorials and graphics in the "hard sell" outside of school should also learn through a wide use of media in the schools?

For the teacher this fact of visual sophistication should suggest that more complex visual experiences may be introduced at an earlier age than was true a generation or so ago. Evidence shows that young children can learn language and spelling via the typewriter, can interpret still pictures, can learn via instructional television, and can use self-instructional materials, such as programmed instruction. Current study in media emphasizes research in the refinements of a given medium rather than raising the broader question of whether students at all levels can learn from various media. In the same sense, there should be no question of whether a teacher should use a variety of media. The questions are rather *which* medium the teacher should select and *which* conditions should be used to enhance learning; this means it is necessary to refine the teacher's understanding of how learners interpret and use each medium.

Programmed Materials and Computer-Assisted Instruction

The programmed instruction boom of the late 1950's and early 1960's continues at a slower pace, and less emphasis is placed upon the "teaching machines" which was characteristic of the early years of programming. The experience that many kinds of sequenced materials could be presented adequately though "linear" or "scrambled" books seems to have influenced the decreased use of expensive machines. Today, programming focuses upon materials stored in computers and presented through various display devices, in addition to book-type materials. Systems of the computer type range from the simple keyboard controlled by the computer to the more elaborate system in which the computer program also activates the display of pictorial and aural materials to which the learner may respond through a keyboard response system and/or a "light pen" placed on the surface of a cathode ray tube. A computer control provides capabilities to adjust programs to individual learners as they proceed through the lesson, to record their responses for continuous analysis, and to learn about the effectiveness of materials through a systematic control of instructional variables.

It is significant that the application of programming principles to learning materials, whether in book form or through machine-mediated systems, has freed each learner for the attainment of prescribed levels of behavior more in competition with herself/himself than against performance levels of a group. Each learner proceeds to the next step in the program only after having mastered the previous criterion level. Thus freed from the restrictions and pressures of learning in groups, the student may proceed at a rate more commensurate with individual abilities and background.

Programmed materials are not, however, the panacea; there have been some problems. There is evidence of boredom where materials are too minutely structured. The better learners, especially, may require materials with larger steps for acquiring information. Another problem is that the very process of programming is time-consuming and costly. There is also some question about how tightly material must be organized into subparts, since research indicates that some kinds of materials may be loosely programmed in prose form, using interspersed questions.

There is concern about the effects of programmed instruction upon learner creativity. Some evidence suggests that creativity may be enhanced by self-pacing, by self-administration of the program, by learner choice of paths and materials, by flexible kinds of feedback, by rewarding deviant responses, by using large steps, and by using actual problems which must be solved in their entirety.

Film Loops

Another more recent development is the continuous film loop, silent or with sound, usually 8mm, available in cartridges with capacities of about four minutes to one-half hour showing time. These cartridges are easily inserted in the appropriate slot of the proper projector, and when the power is switched on, the film appears on a rear screen built into the projection unit. Some projectors allow adjustments for both rear-screen projection and projection on a wall or screen.

An apparent advantage of the film loop is its ease of use by either the teacher or the learner. The latter may use the loop projector very easily in a carrel in the library or in any corner of the school that is convenient to a power outlet. As a self-instructional device, the film loop has the obvious advantages that it is easily handled, even by young learners, and that it can be used repeatedly for as long as the learner needs to view for complete understanding.

Remote-Access Equipment

Another recent development makes information readily accessible to learners through the use of telephone-type dialing or push-button instruments, which are usually installed in locations remote from the source of information. This equipment will play back recorded materials upon demand of the learner when she/he activates the appropriate sequence of numbers to start the playback mechanism. Most frequently this equipment retrieves aural materials. Less frequently, but completely within the capability of most remote-access equipment, the system provides retrieval of visual materials which may be stored as slides, films, or videotapes and are available to the learner via a television receiver which has been built into the learning station. Typical installations provide earphones at each location. The advantages of remote-access information-retrieval systems are obvious. Less clear are the types of materials best suited for retrieval purposes, particularly in terms of information sequencing, cues for listening, and built-in techniques requiring learner responses.

Television

Instructional television has been used in the public schools for more than a decade. General experience has shown that the more completely a school system becomes involved in the use of television on a systemwide basis to solve a major problem, such as upgrading instruction, the greater is its acceptance and use for certain kinds of learning. There are still problems, however, in providing proper intercommunication between the learner and the television teacher. Mechanical systems which permit two-way conversation between the television teacher and students at locations remote from the teacher have not as yet provided satisfactorily the easy two-way communication necessary for the adjustment of the television presentation to the individual questioner. The pragmatic solution to this problem has been provision for "feed-back" in the classroom through techniques in which the regular classroom teacher prepares the learner to view the television program and to participate in appropriate follow-up activities. In some kinds of television programs it has been found that requiring overt response during the program has proved effective, particularly with young children engaging in simpler kinds of learning, such as rhythm exercises in music. By and large, however, television programs are treated in much the same way as a motion picture shown in the classroom—supplementary techniques are used for directed observation. Research has shown that television programs are more effective when they pay attention to such details as clear organization, simplicity of presentation, opportunities for practice, motivating techniques, and knowledge of results. Much more research is needed, however, to capitalize on the unique contributions of pictorialized materials (including television) and to determine the best kinds of instruments to evaluate learning promoted via these means. The practice of using visuals for conveying information and details in the lesson and then testing on the verbal content exclusively has tended to diminish the importance of visuals in learning. In other words, learners who are tested mainly on the verbal content of a lesson will tend to pay attention to words and not to pictures. This suggests that the classroom teacher who uses television instruction or other types of visual media should analyze very carefully whether the testing procedures are appropriate for the type of learning medium used.

Video Tape Recorder

Of more recent origin than the use of television itself has been the development of the portable video tape recorder, now within the cost limits of most schools. This equipment can virtually eliminate the problem of synchronizing broadcast television with class schedules. Simply by acquiring a video tape of the program, or by taping it during the broadcast for later use, the teacher may fit the program into the proper sequence of events. Video tapes have also allowed repetitive use of programs where replay is necessary for fixing learning and for removing misperceptions. Used with a remote-access system, video tapes also allow individuals to view television programs privately.

Another very important advantage of the video tape recorder is in its use for recording teacher and pupil performances. Its use for documenting teaching behaviors of student teachers is already becoming common. Experienced teachers also are using the video tape recorder for private analyses of their own performances.

FUNCTIONS OF MEDIA

Media in their many forms provide the learner with "experience" about the global environment. The bulk of the learner's experience in school tends to be of a vicarious nature, except in some laboratory situations. Much of learning is presented as representations of real life, either because real life is inaccessible or because of the nature of the content, e.g., events which occurred in the past.

One approach to analyzing media potentials for instruction is to assume that teaching is essentially a process of communication and that media may be regarded as avenues for communication. It is clear that learners perceive the world only to the degree permitted by their senses and to the extent that their so-called "cognitive maps" and general intelligence permit them to comprehend and organize what they experience through those senses. For example, it is obvious that a myopic child with uncorrected vision will perceive fewer details of things she/he sees than the child with normal vision. The same may be suggested for restrictions in all the other senses. This means, of course, that the teacher must not expect that simply presenting materials in various forms ensures that the child has the same perception of the material as the teacher. The teacher must discover by questioning techniques what the learner does perceive; the questions should be so structured that to respond, the learner must use the symbols or language she/he is expected to associate with the material. This practice with the associated symbols will provide insights for the teacher in analyzing learner capabilities and in setting learning sequences. Some researchers have reached the conclusion that while careful attention to the sequencing of appropriate materials for the learner is an extremely important task, the extreme individual differences that show up when learners are asked to respond individually to materials indicate that analysis of learners' capabilities is even more important. Teachers need to know a great deal about each learner's capabilities and levels of competence. The hypothesis has been suggested that lack of readiness in learners might actually be the absence of necessary prerequisite competencies and that lack of physical and developmental maturation may be due to the lack of relevant prior learning experiences. A great contribution of media is in providing these prerequisite experiences.

CHARACTERISTICS OF MEDIA

The actual determination of which medium to choose is not easy. For learners who can read at a satisfactory level, for example, it appears that one cannot generalize as to whether the medium should be a picture, spoken or printed words, or sounds. The well-educated adult and the more sophisticated student may learn equally well by hearing or reading. Any teacher serious about the use of media will face questions about the interactions of intelligence, reading ability, age, and content difficulty of the material as these influence the effectiveness of a given medium. These interrelationships are not clearly spelled out at the present.

One might conclude that placing media according to their characteristics on an arbitrary scale or continuum from concrete to abstract automatically means that as one proceeds towards the abstract one should assume also that, for all cases, the more abstract the medium, the more difficult it is for the learner to understand it. This may seem true when one considers the use of a photograph of an object and the use of a line drawing of that same object. One might expect that the photograph would be easier to understand. The crucial question in this instance, as in the selection of any medium, concerns the purpose for which the photograph was intended. If the intention is to observe internal relationships of parts, for example, a photograph of the external surfaces of an object will be less effective than a drawing of that object showing internal views. It appears that the important question the teacher must ask in selecting a photograph is, What are its unique capabilities in comparison to a line representation? Where visuals do not serve a prescribed function, they may distract and interfere.

Where color is not significant to the object or message, it appears not to be crucial to learning. Where motion is not required, one might question the need for a motion picture. These types of problems are important, even though they seem to be within the realm of the obvious. More subtle areas of concern are the influences of such things in media as redundancy of information; the effectiveness of labels and cueing devices; the arrangement of items in a graphic; precision phrasing in film commentary; types of introductions and summaries; details of size and shape of objects; and the interrelationships of objects within frames of filmstrips.

One must conclude that there is actually little evidence that given media contribute to more or better learning than other media under all circumstances; there is evidence that, given favorable conditions, pupils can learn from any instructional medium now available.

MULTIMEDIA PRESENTATIONS

Sometimes questions are raised about the effectiveness of multi-media presentations to learners in groups. The assumption for such use is that the variability among learners in a group requires the use of multimedia presentations as a kind of broad-gauge approach to teaching. To reach all learners simultaneously it is deemed important to provide something for everyone: something verbal, for those facile in verbal communications, and, for the less verbal, media that are less abstract. The term *multimedia* can mean either the use of media in a sequential arrangement or the use of various media presented simultaneously, as in the projection of several images on multiple screens. Multimedia teaching appears to have many merits and should not be minimized where there has been a prior determination that each medium has something to contribute to each member of the group. On the other hand, the simultaneous display of media and the sequencing of the presentation raises questions about competition for attention among media. Take the case of the simultaneous display of three projected images on a divided screen. Even with proper directions, where should the learner turn her/his attention? Does the display of several images simultaneously cause competition for attention which may obviate the effect intended? Research in this area suggests that there may be competition among media which defeats the purposes of the presentation. A human being's sensory mechanism seems to be selective in attending to the various stimuli which are presented simultaneously.

MEETING LEARNING OBJECTIVES

To be used effectively, media must be appropriate for learning objectives. This requires a specification of learning goals in terms that are explicit descriptions of learner behavior, and that are observable and measurable.

Teaching Attitudes

Research has shown that attitudes can be influenced positively by various media, especially films. For young children who have not yet formed the prejudices and biases of adults, the film offers an excellent way to shape desirable attitudes and beliefs. For older learners, including adolescents, the task is more difficult and a combination of emotional appeal and reason is important. On the other hand, the emotional effects of dramatic or traumatic types of films upon learners is well known. Some of the more traumatic films, such as gruesome scenes from automobile accidents, evoke effects which sometimes are of long duration. In general, media research has shown that emotional involvement of some kind in the experience is important and that redundancy or reinforcement of the experience is necessary for lasting changes in attitudes.

Teaching for Understanding

The major purpose of teaching for understanding may be expressed as the development of learner ability to see relationships. This kind of learning can be structured more exactly than affective learning. The time-worn sequence of introduction, presentation of the medium, and follow-up is still applicable. Current research in media, however, indicates that the teacher should focus upon the explicit statement of behavioral objectives. Instead of stating objectives in general terms, such as "understanding 'due process of law,' 'the process of osmosis,' 'the causes of the Civil War,' 'the water-cycle,' or 'our community helpers,'" the statement should be narrower in scope. "Understanding the water cycle" would be stated as "explaining the steps in the water cycle" or "explaining the meaning and function of evaporation and condensation."

Applying this explicitness, one would select media to meet *specific* needs, e.g., to supply particular information, to show exact procedures, or to pictorialize relationships or details. Film research has shown that the more specific the film can be made to the task prescribed for it, the greater is the possibility for learning.

In choosing materials for developing understanding, it would be wise to select materials which are well organized and which have potential for provoking questions. An open-ended film would be such a material—a film designed for discussion, which documents pertinent circumstances of the problem but offers no solutions.

When concepts to be taught are difficult or complex, research supports a second showing of a film, especially when the material is self-contained and does not lend itself to interruption, like a sound film. With carefully prepared guides as supplements, coupled with a thorough discussion between showings, for example, it is generally not necessary to view a complex film a third time. A need to stress content not emphasized in the earlier viewings might be justification for a third showing.

Learners empathize easily with motion picture content because of motion and other filmic techniques. Static materials, such as still pictures and graphics, present another problem. By their very nature they do not generally have built-in attention getters, as does a film with motion. The task of the teacher, therefore, is to plan attention-getting procedures for static materials. The technique of asking for student interpretations and reactions appears to be very effective.

Teaching Skills

In teaching skills, the psychomotor domain, much the same procedures are applicable as in teaching for understanding. This is true at least of identifying the skill to be achieved, of the steps for achieving the skill, and of stating reasons why the skill is important to acquire. For refinement of performance, however, practice is very important to fix procedures. Here the use of the video tape recorder has proved its worth. Confirming results from early motion picture studies, evidence proves that using the video tape recorder to provide the learner with a moving image of herself/himself performing a particular skill has accelerated achievement and has influenced positively her/his self-confidence and self-image.

IMPROVING THE UNDERSTANDING AND USE OF MEDIA

It is becoming more apparent that for the analysis of media applications to learning, it will be necessary to provide either qualified personnel with responsibilities for this task or released time for teachers. Released time for teachers is a valid suggestion, because the planning of self-instructional sequences requires seemingly inordinate amounts of time. Perhaps the proper approach to this issue is not to talk in terms of released time, but to urge redistributions of the teacher's time, questioning the limited effectiveness of group methods for meeting individual needs. It is unrealistic to expect teachers to develop ungraded, continuous progress approaches to learning without adequate preparation time or sufficient support in obtaining prepared materials and in creating those which must be unique. Progress towards individualizing instruction requires in addition well equipped learning resources centers and qualified support personnel who may assist the teacher not only in the design and sequencing of messages for self-instruction, but also in the creation of proper learning facilities. Such support will also take out of the hands of the teacher the details of producing graphic, photographic, and other materials requiring production skills. To provide anything less can be predicted to block acceleration toward the greater individualization of instruction.

CONCLUSION

What might the future be for the teacher, the learner, and the school in general? The literature on media suggests two options: a *machine-independent* school system or a *machine-dependent* school system.

The test of the *machine-independent* system is to remove all of the machines (i.e., projectors, recorders, computers, teaching machines) and observe what happens to the program. If the program and its activities are not measurably affected by the removal, the system is regarded as dependent primarily upon the teacher as the decision maker, authority, and major dispenser of wisdom. In other words, machines in this system are, by virtue of use, incidental, not necessary parts of the basic program for influencing learner behavior.

In the *machine-dependent* system, the removal of the machines would result in a collapse of the basic structure. In other words, the machines carry part of the teaching load and have equal importance with other components in the system. Typical of machines that can do this are those which support self-instruction. The teacher is a necessary component in this structure but assumes roles more concerned with instructional planning, the preparation of materials and learning experiences, and the evaluation of student progress. The teacher in this system has a great deal of importance, as a "mediated" teacher, exerting a growing proportion of influence for certain kinds of learning through printed and recorded forms of instruction. The basic problem confronting such a system is achieving balance between the teacher and machine-dependent avenues for learning. The evidence from research is that machine-dependent systems have proved their worth for providing kinds of learning which are adaptable to nonteacher forms. The future need is for a greater clarification of the teacher's unique contributions and roles.

Logic, experience, and research results point to a growth of machine-dependent systems. The hope is that teachers will assume a dominant role in giving it direction and in helping to provide the ultimate for each learner through the proper balance between human and nonhuman forms of communication.

Directed Study: A Commitment of School and Home to Learning

by Ruth Strang

School years are the time to acquire basic education. The usual five-hour day does not provide time enough. Education must go on outside the school. One method of continuing education beyond the school day has been to require homework. Homework and guided study are closely related; guided study in school should lead to effective study at home.

What is effective study? What methods are confirmed by research on learning? What methods do students usually use? Where do pupils of different ages and abilities study best—in the regular class, in periods set aside for study, in a study hall, in the library, or at home? If at school, how should their study be supervised, by whom, for what purpose, by what methods? If homework is given, we should ask for what purpose, at what ages, under what conditions? And finally, we should ask the possibly embarrassing question: What results are achieved through homework and supervised study?

SUPERVISED AND GUIDED STUDY

According to modern theories of learning, the pupil should (a) want something, (b) perceive something, (c) do something, and (d) get satisfaction from the learning experience. All of these elements should be present in effective study methods. In other words, learning must become integrated with the individual's purpose. The learner must pay attention and be actively involved. The experience must be accompanied or followed by satisfaction. The modern psychology of learning emphasizes motiviation, problem solving, the role of anxiety, interpersonal relations, meaningfulness, reinforcement of any move in the right direction, goals and expectations, and use of whatever is learned. A list of study methods based on research would include the following:

1. Select, if possible, materials and problems that meet a need or arouse a want, interest, or drive.
2. Place any learning task in its larger setting and in the light of the purposes, values, interests, and reasons for doing it.
3. Set appropriate, immediate, and concrete as well as long-term goals.
4. Start with the simple and concrete, and progress gradually to the more complex skills and abstract concepts.
5. Relate previous knowledge and associations to new learning as part of a total pattern or *Gestalt*. See the common elements; find the underlying principles; and relate the new experience to your own life.
6. Take an active attitude toward the learning; expect success.
7. Relate details in a meaningful sequence or pattern; see facts in their relationships; sense the structure of the whole.
8. Practice a skill in the varied situations in which it is needed to make it relatively permanent and precise.
9. Overlearn important facts and skills. One of the greatest wastes of study time results from stopping before the facts are thoroughly fixed in mind.
10. Put facts and other kinds of learning to use in new situations; this not only aids memory but also extends and expands concepts and generalizations.
11. Obtain evidence of progress and the attainment of goals.

Role of the Teacher

In helping students to study more effectively, the classroom teacher's role is obviously far different from the too prevalent present practice of making an unexplained and unmotivated page assignment to a single text. Such an assignment makes no provision for the wide range of reading ability in every grade and gives pupils no practice in setting their own goals or in learning to read to solve real problems.

Ideally, teacher guidance in study involves (a) understanding of individual students—their stage of development, their idea of themselves, their study processes, what is actually going on in their minds, their readiness for a certain kind of learning; (b) providing appropriate, concrete, challenging materials and suggesting timely topics and realistic practical problems; (c) promoting interpersonal relations that furnish incentives for or social reinforcement of learning; (d) encouraging student initiative in setting their own meaningful goals, finding worthwhile problems, discovering their own best ways of learning; and (e) reinforcing and making students aware of those of their study methods which are effective.

Application of Effective Study Methods

Certain general methods of effective learning may be applied to all subjects. For example, in reading, effective learning takes place when instruction and practice are appropriate to the pupil's present development; the books and other reading material are interesting and worthwhile to her/him; she/he feels a need to read; she/he engages in a progression of reading experiences appropriate to individual level; and she/he is neither allowed merely to mark time nor pushed faster than is comfortable. For upper grades, two reading methods need to be especially emphasized: (a) adjusting one's rate and method of reading to the kind of material and the purpose for which it is read, and (b) applying the Survey Q 3R formula to study-type reading. Read the title, recall previous knowledge and experience related to the topic, consider its personal importance, skim through the material reading headings, key sentences, diagrams, etc. Then:

Q—Raise questions that can be answered by the selection.
R_1—Read to get the answers.
R_2—Review to be sure you have the answers in mind.
R_3—Recite in the form in which you will use the ideas gained.

Trends in Supervised Study

Guided or supervised study has passed through many stages, reflecting various concepts of the classroom teacher's work. When teaching no longer consists chiefly of assigning tasks and hearing recitations, guiding students' study becomes a recognized responsibility of the teacher. It should become an intrinsic part of the teaching process. Learning how to learn is surely as important an outcome of education as the facts learned.

Between 1910 and 1938, various plans of supervised study were proposed. After 1938, supervised study was theoretically less often set apart from teaching, and emphasis was put upon student responsibility for planning.

Many classroom teachers recognize the value of supervised study but do not know how to conduct supervised study periods; their supervision consists merely of keeping order. If they are not given sufficient help, students tend to persist too long in their initial trial-and-error ways. This condition is partly due to failure to analyze study methods and to determine those which are best for students of different mental abilities. Since results of how-to-study courses vary with different classes and different students, schools should favor a selective or differential plan of study-supervision.

STUDY AT HOME

Many strands of educational philosophy and method are woven into homework practices. For many years *memorization* was emphasized. The idea that "keeping the student's nose to the grindstone" disciplines her/his mind has long been cited to justify difficult and disagreeable homework assignments.

The *interest* strand was strengthened by Pestalozzi, who diverted attention away from the child's failure to learn and emphasized the teacher's failure to interest the child and hold her/his attention. While recognizing the imporance of interest, Herbart believed that interest grows out of knowledge. Accordingly, he was concerned that children learn so that they would become interested in further learning.

The *child-activity* strand recognized the importance of pupil initiative and responsibility in learning and emphasized the objective of helping pupils use their out-of-school time wisely. These various strands of educational philosophy are still intertwined in the homework assignments of today.

Objectives of Homework

To make any progress in the solution of the homework problem, we ought first to ask: What ends are to be achieved by home study? Among the objectives frequently given are the following:

1. To stimulate voluntary effort, initiative, independence, responsibility, and self-direction. Able students want homework that poses a problem and gives them a chance to use their own ideas or read the books they want to read. They detest unnecessary drill.

2. To encourage a carry-over of worthwhile school activities into permanent leisure interests. We must guard against homework that usurps after-school hours which students could use more constructively.
3. To enrich the school experience through related home activities.
4. To reinforce school learning by providing the necessary practice, integration, and application. "To do better on their examinations" is the way many pupils express it.
5. To acquaint parents with what the child is learning in school and to invite their help.

Kinds of Homework

Homework assignments may be arranged on a continuum from the extreme of mechanical, routine exercises required of all students to the other extreme of creative projects or experiments undertaken voluntarily by individuals.

How do students feel about homework? Any teacher who has a good relationship with her/his students can find out by asking them to write anonymously on the subject "How I Feel about Homework." Such compositions show that many pupils do not object to working at home on interesting problems. Able learners say they like to write "research" reports, to find arguments on both sides of a question, to solve problems, to memorize selections from great literature. They like to be free to read books of their own choice, to do experiments with home equipment. Their homework should include incentives to critical thinking.

The kind of homework assigned is fully as important as the amount of time spent on it. The values to be achieved through homework determine both the kind and the amount. The students' feelings of strain and annoyance may result more from the kind of homework they are given than from the amount of time it takes.

The kind of homework given by classroom teachers and the kind of studying done by students are also influenced by the kinds of examinations students are expected to pass. If tests stress merely the recall of facts rather than power to use information, students tend to focus their attention on details and the exact wording of passages. If tests call for problem solving and the ability to use facts, students are more likely to read to see relationships, to draw conclusions, and to make generalizations rather than merely to memorize.

The kind of studying done also depends a great deal on the nature of the assignment. Exercises that can be done mechanically encourage copying; they may arouse resentment, especially on the part of the bright students. If the assignment requires a "research" type of reading, the students obtain practice in locating sources of information and extracting the information they need. An assignment that calls for initiative, imagination, and individual effort gives no opportunity to copy and challenges the students to work effectively.

Assignments should be planned so that they require a variety of study methods, thus helping to build a repertory of study skills. Students should also learn to integrate different kinds of study experiences and to develop increasingly the ability to determine the specific approach that is appropriate to a given task.

Conditions Conducive to Effective Home Study

Over 75 percent of 748 sixth-, seventh-, and eight-grade students mentioned the following factors as favorable to home study: (a) having a clear understanding of the assignment, (b) having the necessary materials on hand, and (c) quiet and freedom from interruptions. These conditions prevailed less frequently among the disadvantaged.

Cooperation between parents and teachers is essential to effective home study. Parents' groups often discuss homework. One group systematically discussed three topics: "The Worth of Homework," "The Homework Load," and "Homework and the Home." They then held a joint conference with the classroom teachers. The parents' role they said, was to provide conditions conducive to study and to help the child work out a good study schedule, but not to teach or do the homework.

Effective reading methods are basic to successful study. Instruction in effective methods of reading and study is prerequisite to success in home study. Mature readers have been described as those with wide interests and specific purposes that guide their reading. They have in common a repertory of reading skills which they apply appropriately. They vary their rate with the content and with their purposes. They read with active minds first comprehending what the author says and then relating the ideas to their previous knowledge and experiences. They make inferences and generalizations and apply the knowledge gained through reading to the solution of real problems.

To develop mature reading ability, the teacher plans with the student appropriate ways to study the assignment for the day and takes time to teach certain reading and study skills needed by all students, by a few, or by individuals. The skills may be taught to small groups and to individuals while the rest of the class is beginning to work on the assignment.

Modifications of Homework Policies

For more than 50 years schools have been modifying their homework requirements, usually in the direction of less homework and more practical, interesting, and creative assignments. Some have abolished homework. As a result of partially controlled experiments and informal appraisals of the effects of changes in homework practice, certain recommendations have been made:

1. Development of study skills in the elementary school.
2. Provision of time for other activities.
3. More time for guided study in school.
4. Long-term projects.
5. Less written homework.
6. More student initiative and freedom.
7. More meaningful and useful study.
8. Individualized homework.

Discipline: A Maintenance of a Learning Environment

by William J. Gnagey

One of the reasons for the dismal condition in discipline research concerns the market basket character of the concept itself. If a student disrupts the learning experiences in a classroom, there are myriad directions a concerned teacher might take.

Is the student emotionally upset? Do the student's parents belong to a non-middle-class subculture? Are the student's peer relations tenuous? Could she/he be physically sick? Are negative feelings for parents being projected on the teacher?

In this review we shall limit our discussions to the confines of the classroom and the interaction of the people in that situation. In so doing we are leaving the problem of outside causation to researchers in other fields and are slipping into the shoes of every teacher who is faced with the problem of doing something on the spot when a child misbehaves.

Deviancy is the term we will use for a misbehavior. A deviancy occurs when a student takes actions which are prohibited by the teacher.

A *control technique* has been performed when the teacher has taken some action to put an end to the deviancy. Control techniques may be verbal or nonverbal, punitive or nonpunitive, authoritarian or persuasive; but in the context of this discussion, they are always aimed at causing a deviant to desist from his misbehavior.

Witnesses refers to classmates of the deviant who are audience to, but not targets of, the control technique performed by the teacher.

WHAT ARE SOME TYPES OF CONTROL TECHNIQUES?

Before discussing the implications of the findings of experimental research, we turn to descriptive research for assistance on a very practical problem: What are some control techniques that have proved effective in stopping deviancies in certain situations?

Some Strengthen Self-Control

Jane and Janice are working together on a report at the back of the room. Somehow they have gotten off the track and are conversing and giggling so loudly that many others in the class are distracted. Mr. Johnson must decide what to do.

Teachers frequently have to deal with basically well-behaved students who suffer such momentary lapses in their self-control. Several techniques have been found helpful in this type of situation.

1. *Signals* such as a finger on the lips or a "frowny" shaking of the teacher's head might be all that is required to get the girls quietly back to their report.

2. *Moving nearer* the noisy pair could remind them of the proper classroom decorum.

3. Mr. Johnson might use *humor* as a technique and remark, "I didn't know the Debate Society was meeting back there."

4. The girls' *interest might be boosted* if Mr. Johnson declared, "That's a pretty important report you're writing. May I see how it's coming along?"

5. *Diverting their attention* back to the report, the teacher might ask, "Have you thought of using the new encyclopedia to answer some of your questions?"

6. *Ignoring* the noise for a moment might be Mr. Johnson's choice of technique if he believes that the noise will soon subside by itself.

Each of these techniques has been found to be helpful in supporting a deviant's waning self-control.

Some Reduce Frustration

Since there has been established for some time a firm relationship between frustration and emotional behavior, it should not be surprising that some misbehavior can result from classroom situations in which a student cannot reach her/his goals.

Sam is distracting the whole arithmetic class. Not only is he making ominous sounds under his breath, but he has torn up four successive notebook sheets and crammed the remains into his desk. Miss Sims has to decide how to handle the situation.

1. Some *hurdle help* might quiet Sam down. A little of Miss Sim's time could be well spent helping Sam understand how to compute the answers to the problems that have been harassing him.

2. *Restructuring* might be the appropriate technique for Miss Sims on another day. This time the whole class seems restless and unable to get down to work. The assignment for the day is a review of the multiplication facts for the sevens, eights, and nines. In order to fulfill her objectives, Miss Sims might change the whole situation.

Instead of using the usual workbook review sheets, children could take turns being "teacher" and posing multiplication facts to the group. Any student who gets three combinations correct in a row becomes the new "teacher."

3. As still other teachers have discovered, *temptations must be removed* far away from some pupils or deviancy is bound to be repeated. Miss Sims uses a kind of "wheel of fortune" machine for practice in number combinations. Although it serves its arithmetic functions well, students cannot seem to resist spinning it at other times. Since it emits a loud chattering sound not unlike a stick clattering along a picket fence, Miss Sims removes the temptation to a safe cupboard at the end of each class.

4. The early establishment of *routines* has been effective in reducing deviancies. Passing out papers, collecting notebooks, using the pencil sharpener, going to the lavatory: all these necessary daily activities can be breeding grounds for misbehavior.

5. One technique that might work with Phyllis is called *painless removal*. Phyllis is a girl who very easily loses her temper. In times of stress she may stamp and shout and say things she is sorry for later.

Miss Sims must learn to step in quickly and direct Phyllis to leave the room for a time until she cools off.

6. In some rare instances the teacher may have to use *physical restraint* to prevent a badly overwrought child from hurting herself/himself and others.

7. Ideally a teacher should try to avoid unnecessary frustrations before they arise. This may sometimes be accom-

plished by careful *previewing* of potentially dangerous or overstimulating situations. For several years Miss Potter had taken her fifth-grade class to see a huge hydroelectric plant in operation. Since the roar of the big turbines made communication difficult, pupils had often misheard the guide's directions and had sometimes walked dangerously near some of the giant machines. Others had become so excited that they had run about shouting to one another in a most disorganized manner. Last year the teacher seriously considered cancelling the annual trip.

In response to a suggestion by her principal, Miss Potter and her class took plenty of time before the trip to talk about the noise they would hear and the difficulties that might arise. They worked out a series of hand signals for communicating in the din and practiced using them at recess. Upon returning from the tour, Miss Potter said that it had been the best trip yet.

Some Appeal to Understanding

Frank Carter teaches high school chemistry. The laboratory period presents a number of situations where deviancies might flourish. In one case, Larry couldn't seem to observe the safety precautions concerning the use of acids. Mr. Carter knew that something had to be done.

1. *Power with reason* is one technique that Mr. Carter could use in this situation. Saying to Larry, "You have to treat those acids with respect. You could very easily burn someone badly," might reduce this deviancy markedly.

2. At another time the class came into the laboratory after an exciting class election. No one could seem to settle down to routine procedures. Mr. Carter might then use a *power with cushion* technique that directs the class to get busy but helps them recognize the cause for their behavior. "I know that you are all excited about the election, but we have to get back on the beam."

WHAT IS THE RIPPLE EFFECT?

The familiar declaration, "I'll make an example of you!" attests to the fact that parents and teachers have long

136

taken the Ripple Effect for granted. They have realized that by dealing with the deviancy of one student, they were really dealing with the whole class by proxy. It is as though the effects of a control technique spread out from the deviant like concentric wavelets of influence to those classmates who are witnesses to the episode.

Since the Ripple Effect may greatly increase the number of students influenced by a control technique, each deviancy episode takes on new significance. A knowledge of the factors that produce variations in this effect are of paramount importance to the teacher who wishes to reduce the amount of deviancy in her/his classroom.

HOW DO TECHNIQUES INFLUENCE THE RIPPLE EFFECT?

Although we have previously taken space to describe various control techniques, we emphasized those measures that have been effective in influencing a deviant to desist. We now turn to experimental evidence concerning the impact of some of these techniques upon the Ripple Effect.

Let us agree that the major reason for performing a given control technique is to improve the learning situation. Deviancies are stimuli that may evoke responses that compete with those to be learned. It is possible, however, to use some control technique that may stop a deviancy but simultaneously increase the level of behavior disruption for all the witnesses.

The problem then becomes, "What are some characteristics of control techniques that reduce the chances that witnesses will become deviants and that will not produce unnecessary distractions from their studies?"

Threats Exert an Influence

Research studies show that in general, highly emotional threats produce a great deal of distracting behavior-disruption among students who witness the episode. Nail-biting, shifting in seats, chewing pencils, looking around, and so forth are all behaviors that increase after a rough and threatening technique has been used. What is even more important, these rough, emotional techniques do not lower the number of later deviancies that witnesses perform.

137

Additional findings indicate that a teacher's use of threatening control techniques causes witnesses to lower their estimation of her/his helpfulness, likeability, and fairness. Students do, however, tend to rate a teacher higher on her/his ability to control a class of "tough kids." Treatment of deviancies by rough control techniques also causes the witnesses to raise their estimates of the seriousness of those infractions.

Clarity Produces Results

Verbal commands such as "Hey, cut that out!" have very low clarity. They do not tell who the deviant is, what the deviancy is, or what to do to stop it.

A teacher who reacts to a disturbing noise by commanding, "Jim, stop drumming on your desk and get busy on those arithmetic problems," has performed a control technique of great clarity.

Researchers find that as a teacher increases the clarity of her/his verbal discipline, witnesses are less likely to become deviants. At the same time, clear control techniques do not increase behavior disruption.

Firmness Influences Ripple

A firm control technique may have one or more of several characteristics conveying an "I mean it" quality to the teacher's action. A serious, businesslike tone of voice, walking closer to the deviant, or continuing to look at the deviant until she/he desists: all of these contribute firmness to a teacher's efforts at control. A bland or plaintive suggestion such as "I wish you people would pay attention," has low firmness. It may even verge on helpless entreaty.

Investigators find that increasing firmness of a control technique (as long as it does not become rough and excessively threatening) increases the conformance of both the deviant and witnesses who are oriented toward or interested in the deviancy at the time of the event.

Focus Affects Control

"I hear noise in the back of this room. Mrs. Cooper doesn't like noisy children in her room." This is one example of what researchers call an *approval-focused* control technique. It depends for its effect upon the relationship between the teacher and the students.

A *task-focused* technique dealing with the same deviancy might sound like this: "I hear noise in the back of this room. We will never finish learning how to do square root if that din continues."

Findings indicate that task-focused control techniques elicit more desirable student reactions than do approval-focused efforts. Witnesses to task-focused techniques not only raise their estimates of the teacher's skill in handling children, but they gain in interest in the subject matter being taught.

HOW DOES THE DEVIANT INFLUENCE THE RIPPLE EFFECT?

Witnesses who see a deviant submit to a teacher's control technique rate that teacher as "more capable of handling kids" than when the deviant responds in a defiant manner.

Submissive deviant responses also cause witnesses to rate the teacher as "more expert" than when deviants defy the teacher. It is as though successfully handling a deviancy increases the overall prestige of the teacher.

Classmates who witness submissive responses to control techniques judge those techniques to be fairer than do those who see deviants defy a teacher. The general feelings of the witnesses seem to parallel those acted out by the deviant.

If we are to predict accurately the influence of any deviant's response, we must know something about her/his prestige among the witnesses. Investigators have shown that the reaction of a deviant is far more influential if classmates hold her/him in high regard.

HOW DO WITNESSES INFLUENCE RIPPLE?

Research evidence indicates that a deviancy episode is perceived much differently by students who are highly motivated to learn a subject than by their less interested classmates. Highly motivated students rate deviancies as more disturbing and more serious. They see control techniques as more fair and take the teacher's side in conflicts with class deviants.

Students with low motivation to learn a subject see their teacher's control techniques as angry and punitive. They describe these actions in teacher-approval-focused rather than task-focused terms.

Students' motivation also seems to influence their perception of the teacher. When asked to describe their teacher, students who are highly motivated use more task-relevant descriptions. They discuss the teacher's competence in explaining material, the quality of homework assignments, and the like. Low-motivated students emphasize nontask teacher attributes such as fairness and other personal qualities.

Finally, students who are highly motivated to learn pay more attention to the learning task and behave themselves even better after a control technique has been performed.

There Are Practical Implications

After examining the research findings concerning the influence of witness characteristics on the Ripple Effect, one might come to the following conclusions:

1. The more interesting a subject can be made, the more effective a teacher's control efforts become. Data from other areas indicate a lower incidence of deviancy in interesting classes. This research, however, associates interest with more efficient control of those deviancies that do occur.

2. If a teacher must choose between being liked and organizing an interesting course of study, the latter should more strongly influence her/his control of classroom misbehavior.

CAN GOOD BEHAVIOR BE LEARNED AND UNLEARNED?

A number of psychologists have been treating misbehavior problems as special cases in faulty learning. Just as a student may learn to type using an incorrect finger placement, so another pupil may learn social behavior that is disruptive to the classroom.

Basically, a teacher must stimulate students to perform acceptable classroom behavior and make it worth their while. Psychologists who can exert nearly complete control over their subjects' environment have brought about startling improvements in their behavior.

"Good" behavior is taught by withholding all but the minimal need gratifications until the acceptable behaviors are performed. Deviancies are ignored.

These procedures have been successful over a wide range of behavior problems, from infant toilet training to lack of cooperation among pupils of school age.

Rewards Must Be Individualized

As with so much of teaching, a generalization is only a beginning point. To say that rewarded behaviors persist, immediately raises another question: "What is rewarding to the student?"

The kindergarten teacher who says, "I like the way Jimmie is sitting up straight," is doling out a piece of approval to reinforce good posture.

Can you visualize the consternation that would ensue, however, if a high school Spanish teacher used the same technique nine years later! Jimmie would be embarrassed, and his classmates would taunt him mercilessly about his goody-goody posture and about being the teacher's "fair-haired boy." The kinds of events that are rewarding depend heavily upon the developmental stage of a student.

But the veteran teacher who has worked with junior high school youngsters long enough to eliminate such "developmental mistakes" still has one more step to take. She/he must know what events are most rewarding to each student in the class. Only after a teacher can list a few situations that are highly pleasing to a certain student can she/he begin to reinforce preferred classroom behavior efficiently.

Unrewarded Behavior Disappears

Recent research abounds with reports of behavior improvement by means of the extinction of "bad habits." We have pointed out that good behavior is learned because it is gratifying or can be made so by the teacher. The opposite also is true.

Actions that do not bring a student closer to one or more of her/his goals tend to disappear. Even such violent misbehavior as a tantrum will disappear when all results that formerly made it worthwhile are withheld.

The problem is once more that the teacher, unlike the experimental psychologist, does not have complete control over a student's reinforcements.

Studies of various schedules of reinforcement show clearly that if a deviancy is reinforced even once in a while by some agent beyond the teacher's control, it may be repeated over and over again. But research on extinction clearly shows that if a teacher can arrange the classroom so that deviant behaviors are devoid of rewards, their chances of being repeated drop toward zero.

DOES PUNISHMENT IMPROVE BEHAVIOR?

Punishment, as we shall use the term, differs from *restitution.* If a pupil is made to restate a discourteous comment in a more polite fashion, we would not term it punishment, but restitution. Before a student can be expected to repeat "good" behavior, she/he must perform the desirable behavior and be rewarded for it.

The punishment of which we speak here might be called retributive. When a teacher inflicts pain or discomfort on a student because the student has been "bad" and "deserves it," this is retributive punishment. When fear of re-experiencing unpleasantness becomes the major reason for a pupil's avoiding deviancy, the technique may be termed *punitive.*

Teachers who make generous use of punitive control techniques often defend their actions by saying, "It may not agree with the psychology books, but it works." What the teacher usually means is that the deviancy doesn't recur or spread. Research corroborates the principle that the longer the duration of a punishment, the longer the punished response will be suppressed.

But punishment works on other aspects of behavior also. Studies have shown repeatedly that organisms learn to fear the people and objects that are close to them when they are punished. In cases of repeated severe punishment, children may learn to react with fear to the teacher, the classroom, the text, and the subject. Since this reaction may spread to other teachers' classes and subjects, it can be a very high price to pay for deviancy suppression.

ACKNOWLEDGMENTS

The articles in this book have been adapted from reports in NEA's *What Research Says to the Teacher* series as follows:

"Physical Fitness: A Cornerstone of Learning" from *Physical Fitness* by Paul Hunsicher

"Mental Fitness: A Prime Factor in Learning" from *Mental Fitness* by Robert F. Peck and James V. Mitchell, Jr.

"Anxiety: A Deterrent to Effective Learning" from *Anxiety as Related to Thinking and Forgetting* by Frederick F. Lighthall

"Motivation: An Initiation to the Learning Process" from *Motivation in Teaching and Learning* by Don E. Hamachek

"Creativity: An Extension of the Learning Parameters" from *Creativity* by E. Paul Torrance

"The Group: An Asset or a Liability to Learning?" from *Group Processes in Elementary and Secondary School* by Louis M. Smith

"Group Interaction: A Significant Force in Learning" from *Understanding Intergroup Relations* by Jean D. Grambs

"Disadvantaged Groups: A Special Challenge" from *Teaching the Disadvantaged* by Gertrude Noar

"The Sensory Environment: A Building Block to Learning" from *Sensory Factors in the School Learning Environment* by G. F. McVey

"Listening: A Particular Sensory Concern" from *Listening* by Stanford E. Taylor

"Media: A Current and Future Environment" from *Educational Media* by Gerald M. Torkelson

"Directed Study: A Commitment of Home and School to Learning" from *Guided Study and Homework* by Ruth Strang

"Discipline: A Maintenance of a Learning Environment" from *Controlling Classroom Misbehavior* by William J. Gnagey